KT-237-820

A YEAR *of* WELL BEING

This Modern Books edition published in 2015 by
Elwin Street Productions

Conceived and produced by
Elwin Street Limited
3 Percy Street
London W1T 1DE
www. elwinstreet.com

Additional text: Bridget Grenville-Cleave, Anna May and Gillian Whitaker

ISBN: 978-1-906761-56-1

Printed and bound in Singapore

Disclaimer: The advice, recipes and exercises in this book are intended as a personal guide to healthy living. However, this information is not intended to provide medical advice and it should not replace the guidance of a qualified physician or other healthcare professional. Decisions about your health should be made by you and your healthcare provider based on the specific circumstances of your health, risk factors, family history and other considerations. See your healthcare provider before making major dietary changes or embarking on an exercise programme, especially if you have existing health problems, medical conditions or chronic diseases. The author and publishers have made every effort to ensure that the information in this book is safe and accurate, but they cannot accept liability for any resulting injury or loss or damage to either property or person, whether direct or consequential and howsoever arising.

Picture credits
Shutterstock: Vilor pp. 5, 26, 46, 62, 76, 100, 116, 126, 146, 157, 172, 190, 206, 222, 229, 244, 264, 276, 294; Scisetti Alfio p. 10; Deep OV p. 12; My Good Images p. 15; Perutskyi Petro p. 19; Joanna Dorota p. 20; marco mayer p. 22; EM Arts p. 33; Mykola Mazuryk p. 39; Olga Danylenko p. 41; Victoria Martin p. 42; Volosina pp. 45, 134; topseller p. 48; Kati Molin pp. 53, 65; Robyn Mackenzie p. 55; jocic p. 56; B. and E. Dudzinscy p. 59; viki2win p. 67; Igor Strukov p. 73; Elena Schweitzer p. 75; moomsabuy p. 81; Olga Lyubkina p. 85; andreasnikolas p. 89; iravgustin p. 93; Bohbeh p. 95; Anteromite p. 102; oksana2010 p. 105; Natalia Klenova p. 107; AN NGUYEN p. 121; Natalia Van Doninck p. 122; nature photos p. 125; Svetlana Romantsova p. 130; Lipowski Milan p. 133; Pawel Kazmierczak p. 136; Aprilphoto p. 139; DUSAN ZIDAR p. 140; nito pp. 142, 219; KIM NGUYEN p. 148; JIANG HONGYAN p. 150; Hanna Alandi p. 155; Shots Studio p. 159; marlooo p. 163; Crepesoles p. 166; Saikom p. 168; Nneirda p. 171; baibaz p. 175; In Tune p. 177; Smit p. 181; omphoto p. 184; EBFoto p. 187; Yasonya p. 192; freya-photographer p. 197; sarkao p. 199; Sponner p. 201; bonchan p. 203; Africa Studio p. 208; JanBussan p. 211; Dionisvera p. 212; Magdanatka p. 217; Stefan Petru Andronache p. 221; surassawadee p. 225; Roman Samokhin p. 227; Chursina Viktoriia p. 232; Stokkete p. 235; Ivaschenko Roman p. 238; Dmitriy Raykin p. 243; Zelenskaya p. 246; vovan p. 250; Nattika pp. 253, 297; PHOTOCREO Michal Bednarek p. 255; jukurae p. 256; l i g h t p o e t p. 261; Irina Rogova p. 266; Showcake p. 269; Tami Freed p. 271; Nata-Lia p. 279; photastic p. 281; Diana Taliun p. 283; Julia Zakharova p. 287; f9photos p. 288; lapas77 p. 291; TAGSTOCK1 p. 299

iStock: pavlinec pp. 6, 83; Liuhsihsiang p. 9; AlasdairJames pp. 17, 29, 91; Muenz p. 31; Scrambled p. 51; shawn_hempel p. 69; photomaru p.113; MariuszBlach p. 119; dionisvero p. 231

Getty images: T-Pool / STOCK4B p.34

Alessandra Spairani: pp. 96, 113

Alamy: Biglife p. 153

A YEAR *of* WELL BEING

DR PATRICIA MACNAIR

DR ILONA BONIWELL

CONTENTS

INTRODUCTION

More of us the world over are living longer – the number of centenarians in the UK has more than quadrupled in the last 30 years. According to the first Australian centenarian study (2010), while genetics do play a part, a healthy lifestyle and a positive outlook are better determinants of long life. And, happily, we live in an age where information about how to improve the quality of our lives is readily available.

This essential volume presents a year's worth of advice for improving your wellbeing, touching on the factors that most influence and enrich human health and happiness. With each day comes a new activity, a new way of thinking or a new source of inspiration. As you journey through your year of wellbeing, you will see how simple changes, when added up, can have a significant impact on your relationships, intelligence, environment and physical and mental health. Based on the latest scientific studies and academic research, these tips are designed to be practical and simple to incorporate into your life.

The book also takes a keen focus on mindfulness – a state of mind increasingly recognised by health professionals for its role in wellbeing. Mindfulness is all about being attuned to your own body and mind, a focus of attention that is the cornerstone to psychological acceptance, control and contentment. This book contains techniques for understanding and practising mindfulness, including exercises to help heighten your awareness of 'being'.

So take responsibility for your health and happiness and find the person you're meant to be.

HOW TO USE THIS BOOK

This book is divided into the four seasons with a simple and practical piece of advice for each day of the year. Each season also contains the following features:

Health and Juice Days: Delicious and healthy recipes that use seasonal fruits and vegetables , plus refreshing and energising juice recipes

Daily Inspiration: Memorable quotes about wellbeing from famous cultural figures

Relax and Unwind: Deep breathing exercises to calm your nerves and put you into a mindful state

Stretch: Stretching exercises that lengthen your muscles, improve your flexibility and correct your posture

Train the Brain: Challenging and fun puzzles and teasers to strengthen your brain.

This book encourages you to make relatively small changes that, when embraced, can impact your life in a big way. It's important though to keep a couple of things in mind as you take on your year of wellbeing:

- When giving up things or breaking habits, focus on the positive benefits that will come from doing this.
- Everyone is unique so do not put too much pressure on attaining a certain result. Some changes may be easier for you to make than others. Further to that, some days will be healthier than others, so be forgiving on yourself if you have an unhealthy day. The key is being committed and enthusiastic about making changes to better your health and quality of life.

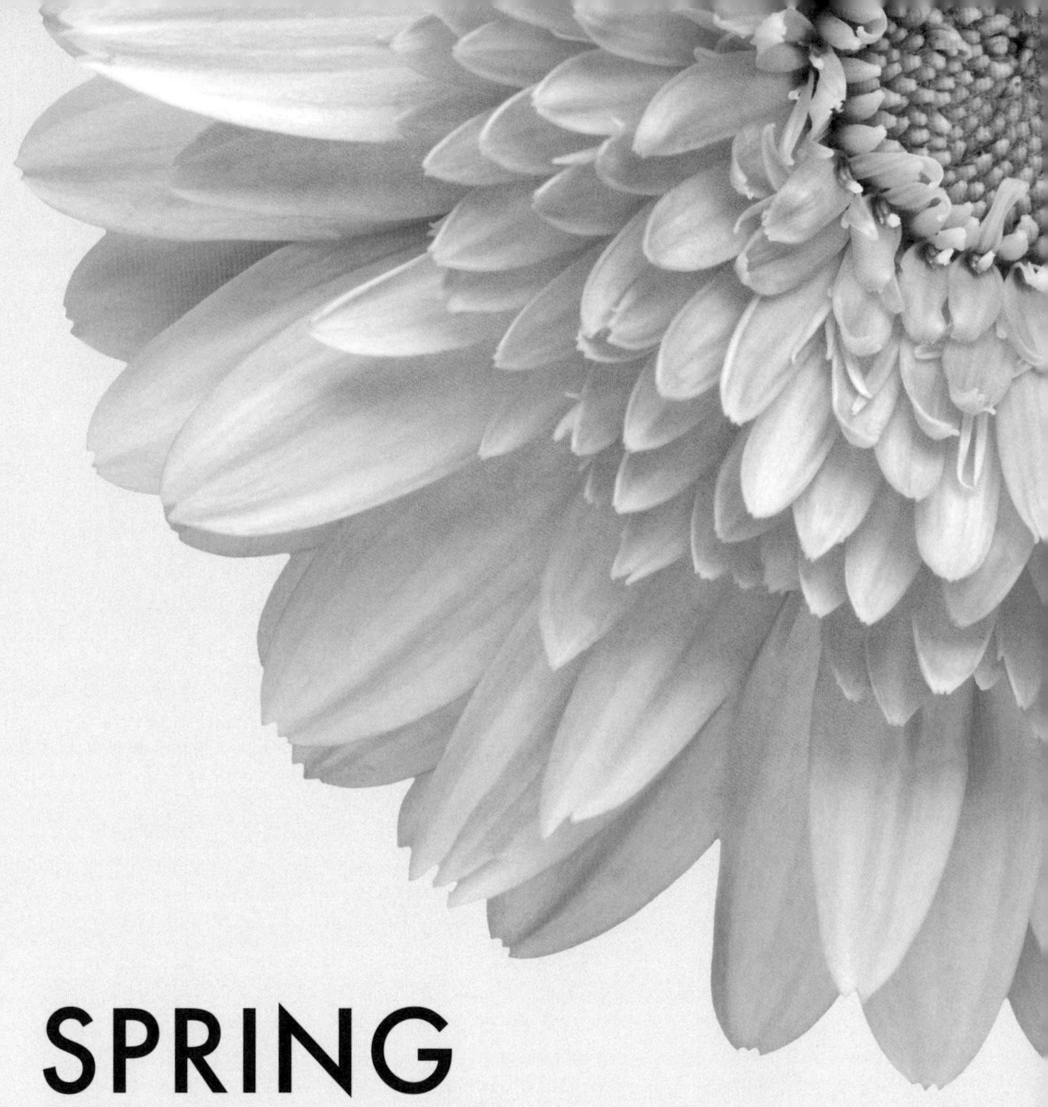

SPRING

Spring is a time for new beginnings, the perfect season to start taking positive steps to improve your wellbeing. Now's the time to get your mind and body back into shape after enduring months of darkness and heavy winter carbs.

GET IN TOUCH WITH NATURE

After a hectic week at the office – full of meetings, presentations, emails, phone calls and eating on the go, not to mention hours of commuting – it can be a huge relief to escape to the countryside. Studies show that contact with nature can have an immense effect on your happiness.

Natural spaces have beneficial effects on psychological wellbeing, such as reducing the mental fatigue caused by tasks that require deep concentration. Views of greenery have also been proven to have a positive effect on physical health, for example, by reducing blood pressure.

One theory to explain why we are so drawn to, and soothed by, natural landscapes – particularly plants, flowers and water – is that they contributed to our survival as early humans.

Happily, natural beauty can be found almost everywhere, even in cities. A good park can transport you away from the concrete and traffic sounds of even the largest metropolis. Take a stroll along a waterfront. Find some good spots for watching sunsets or gazing at stars. Plan weekend trips to nature reserves or parks. Fitting in time to spend with nature can be difficult, but if you actively look for natural beauty, you will be justly rewarded.

02

KICK OUT THE CLUTTER

Most people feel stressed and oppressed when faced with chaos. Whether the cause is a jumble of material possessions, a muddle of outstanding debts or the aftermath of a difficult relationship, the stress of clutter can cause the pulse rate and blood pressure to rise to unhealthy levels. Clutter doesn't appear overnight and won't go away quickly either, so set aside time to organise your life. Follow these easy tips for a better life:

- Break down the mess into small chunks. Tackle just one room, one cupboard or one drawer at a time.
- Get rid of stuff you haven't touched in years – take it to a charity shop, give it to a friend or have a carboot sale.
- Reorganise your storage space so that you can put things away and then easily find them again.

03

HAVE A STRETCH

Stretching is an important part of any exercise programme, although it is usually the most underrated part. It is important to allow the connective tissue surrounding your muscle fibres to lengthen, thereby enabling your body to support more vigorous activity. It can also improve your posture, reduce the risk of injury and increase relaxation.

Try to do some form of stretching every day, ideally morning and evening as well as before any form of exercise. We've included three stretches in every season for you to incorporate into your daily routine.

BE CURIOUS

Curiosity killed the cat, or so the saying goes. But research shows that, actually, inquisitive people tend to be more creative, feel less stress and boredom and relish challenges. Curious children enjoy school more, have better relationships with their teachers and are confident that they will succeed in life.

So can you actively develop your sense of curiosity? There is no scientifically proven way to do this; however, here are some good places to start:

- Love to learn. Viewing learning and education as opportunities for fun and discovery will naturally encourage your curiosity and help you expand your mind.
- Be open. Learn about recent history by talking to people who have lived through it, rather than by simply reading about it, so you can understand different perspectives. This may stimulate both short- and long-term curiosity.
- Find an activity that means something to you personally. This will fuel your need to know, leading to an upward spiral of positive emotion.

05

REST YOUR EYES

Our eyes are not designed to cope with prolonged close-up work, such as staring at a computer screen. This can make the eyes feel gritty and uncomfortable, or lead to headaches and blurred vision. There are several things you can do to reduce the risk of eye strain when using your computer:

- Glance up briefly at regular intervals. Move your eyes from side to side, or gaze at a distant object, to break the intense focus on one point.
- Every 45 minutes, take a break and do something different. Try to avoid digital devices altogether during this time.
- Remember to blink often. When you blink, your eyelids spread tear film over the surface of the eyes to keep them moist and sweep away dust and dirt particles.

06

EAT REGULARLY

Eating regular meals will maintain your blood glucose at a steady level and help to keep you in peak mental form throughout the day. Studies show that eating regularly benefits short-term memory, improves rapid information processing and makes possible more focused and sustained attention.

Rather than having three large meals a day, divide them into five to six smaller meals and snacks. In this way, your body's energy levels are constantly being replenished, and it will prevent you from overindulging at main meals.

07

PRACTISE YOGA

The combination of movement, breathing and meditation that makes up yoga practice helps to exercise the body and calm the mind. There is also evidence that it can improve cognitive function.

In 2008, Indian yoga experts looked at the effect of yoga on cognitive abilities in women with menopausal symptoms. They divided 120 women into two groups and asked them to take part in a study that would occupy an hour a day, five days a week for two months. One group practised breathing exercises, sun salutations and cyclic meditation, while the other did a set of simple physical exercises. At the end of the study, the women in the yoga group had fewer hot flushes and night sweats and less sleep disturbance, as well as noted improvements in memory and concentration.

Most people practise hatha yoga, which uses postures, breathing techniques and meditation to promote a sense of wellbeing. Hatha yoga rests on the notion of balance and the union of opposites ('Ha' means the sun and 'tha' signifies the moon). Varying yoga styles emphasise different approaches, ranging from the meditative Ananda yoga to the highly vigorous Bikram yoga, which really gives you a workout. Ashtanga yoga is a popular choice, a physical option that begins with a sun salutation and is made up of sequences of postures designed to strengthen and purify the nervous system. But there is a range of different yoga styles out there, so you can choose one that matches your needs and preferences.

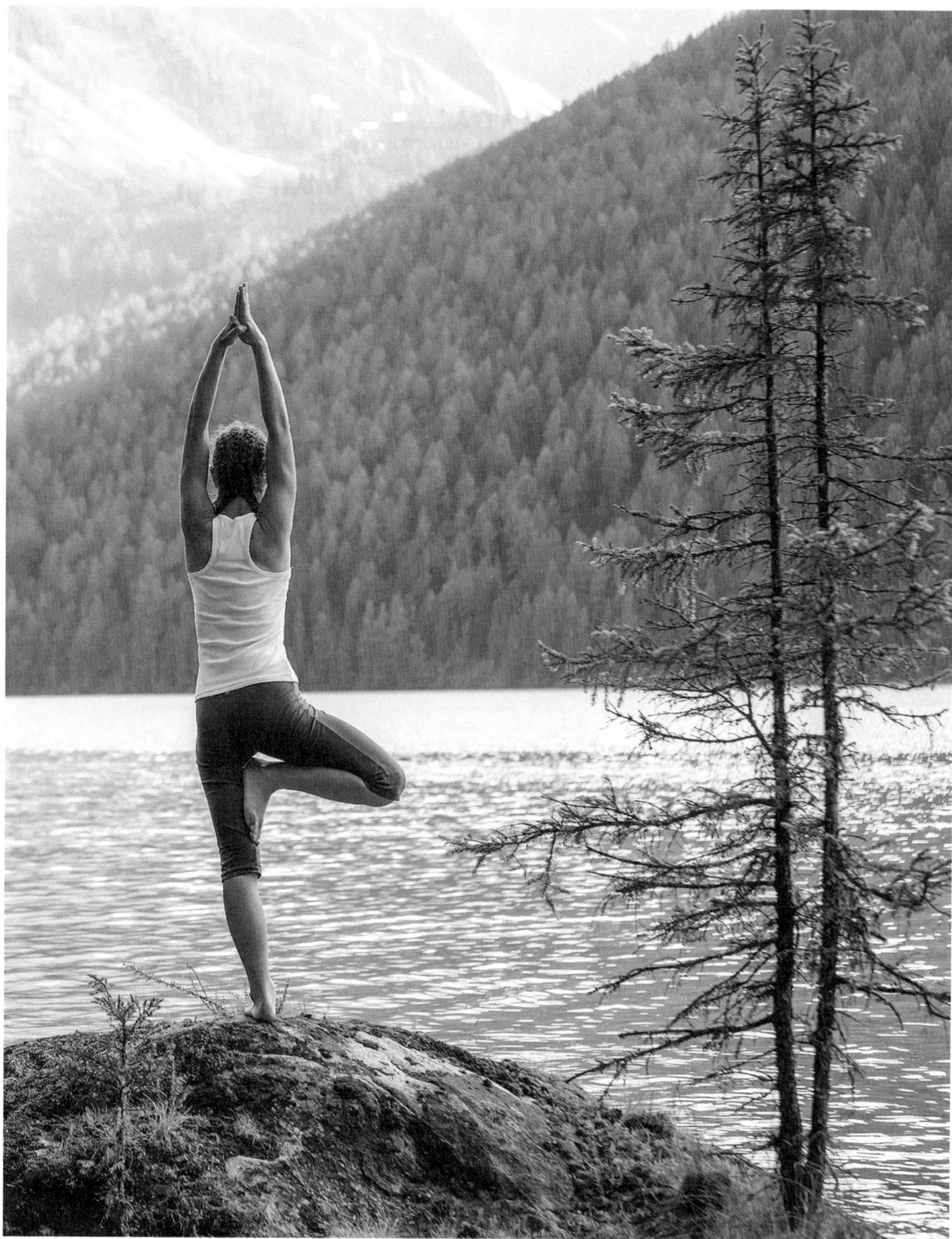

08

PLAY TO YOUR STRENGTHS

People who regularly use one of their personality strengths in a new way every day for a week have higher happiness and lower depression levels in the long term. To identify your own strengths, answer the following questions:

- Think about some everyday things that you enjoy doing – what would you say you enjoy the most and why?
- Thinking back to when you were young, what were your best times? What were you doing?
- What are you doing when you feel most alive and full of energy?

Identifying and building on your strengths will help you value yourself and encourage you to reach your highest potential.

09

DISCOVER ALOE VERA

The aloe vera plant is the source of one of nature's oldest and most effective remedies. Its fleshy leaves can be sliced open to yield a cooling gel that has long been valued for its medicinal properties, especially in the treatment of skin problems.

Aloe vera gel is particularly effective when applied to damaged skin. It aids in the healing of minor burns, sunburn and skin wounds, creating a moisturising barrier against infection. Aloe also dilates the tiny blood vessels known as capillaries, allowing more blood to reach the wound and thereby speeding up healing. Fresh gel from a live leaf is the most potent form, but it is now found in many other products, such as skin lotions, deodorants and cosmetics.

BOOST YOUR ENERGY

Detoxing will put a sparkle back into your eyes, as well as helping you to lose weight and tone up, but the most immediate health benefit you'll notice is a boost in energy.

Eliminate: Start by eliminating from your diet any foods and drinks that are causing your body to feel sluggish or unhealthy, beginning with junk foods, caffeine, sugars and processed foods. Elimination doesn't mean cutting out everything – just the products that are doing your body harm. You could fast or just eat fruit for a day to rebalance your system.

Energise: You'll feel tired at first because your body is going through a withdrawal process and is craving its usual energy boosters, such as sugar, nicotine or carbohydrates. The good news is that it doesn't take too long to eliminate these from your system and you should notice the energising benefits within a few days.

Exercise: Activities that involve slow repetitive movements, such as walking, swimming, yoga or t'ai chi, are all ideal to help your body to relax and rejuvenate.

HAVE REALISTIC AIMS

If you want to make big changes in your life or kick a bad habit, ensure that your aims are realistic. Devise a strategy involving small, positive steps as part of a gradual but steady journey.

Working towards a goal is as important to wellbeing as the attainment of the goal itself, so focus on the journey as much as the destination. A 2009 study at University College London found that it takes an average of 66 days for a new behaviour pattern to become part of someone's regular routine. So give yourself time to adapt to each phase of your new regime and to reassure yourself that the changes are sustainable.

Write a list of your major goals, and beside each goal write down the steps required to achieve it and the timescale needed. Then break down the steps into daily or weekly targets, ready to be ticked off when they have been accomplished. If you want to learn a new language, for example, you could put aside two hours a day or one day a week for concentrated study. The programme may need to be adapted as you move closer to achieving your aims.

LOOK AFTER YOUR LIVER

The liver is one of the body's most important organs. Its main job is to filter and detoxify substances that enter the body: food, nutrients, liquids and oxygen. When it comes to physical wellbeing, your liver resembles the engine of a car; if you don't keep it in good condition, your body simply will not run properly. And, as with a car, the health of your liver depends on how you treat it.

The main preventative measure for liver disease is to drink alcohol only in moderation, and the only way to improve the function of a drink-damaged liver is complete abstinence.

There are a few other steps you can take to keep your liver healthy:

- Have just two to three moderate servings of protein foods a day. These include milk, meat, poultry, fish and pulses.
- Eat foods rich in vitamins C and E, such as oranges, berries, kiwi fruit, peppers and dark green vegetables. They help to protect the liver from potentially damaging free radicals.
- Drink green tea. Also rich in antioxidants, it may enhance the effects of vitamins C and E.
- Take milk thistle supplements. Extracts of the plant protect liver cells, encourage repair of damaged cells and stimulate the growth of new ones.

COOK AT HOME

If you want to eat healthily, it makes sense to cook meals at home. Although it requires a bit more time and effort than resorting to ready meals from supermarkets, it allows you to buy fresh ingredients from trusted suppliers and be sure about their origins.

Using fresh, seasonal ingredients also means that you can forget about the possible health dangers from the large quantities of sugar, salt and other additives found in many processed foods. Plus preparing meals at home can be therapeutic in itself – and the ultimate pleasure is to sit around a table and share a home-cooked meal with family and friends.

14

GET ON YOUR BIKE

Cycling is great exercise, whatever your age. It shapes and tones the thighs and calves, as well as the muscles of the pelvis, while not putting too much strain on your joints. Overall strength, stamina and general muscle power will improve, even in the occasional cyclist. Cycling also puts the heart and lungs through their paces, lowering your resting pulse, blood pressure and blood-fat levels.

Start cycling gently, beginning with short trips, especially if you haven't cycled before or for a long time. Build up your fitness levels by consistently riding twice during the week, slowly increasing the length of time you spend in the saddle.

And while riding, be sure to be safe – use lights and wear a helmet and bright, reflective clothing so that people can see you.

15

SHARE GLAD TIDINGS

Research shows that when you share good news or celebrate an event with others you experience a sense of happiness over and above the happiness associated with the event itself. What's more, the more people you tell, the more your happiness increases. So next time you have a piece of good news, make sure you share it with as many of your friends as possible. And when someone shares their good news with you, be genuinely pleased for them. You'll be making them and yourself happier in the process.

HEALTH DAY: TOFU PAD THAI

Tofu is a great source of protein (especially for vegetarians), low in calories and fat and high in iron and other minerals, as well as very adaptable.

- 400g (14 oz) firm tofu
- 8 tablespoons soy sauce
- 225g (½ lb) dried fine rice noodles
- 1 onion
- 4 cloves garlic
- 85g (½ cup) peanuts
- 2 tablespoons rapeseed oil
- 175g (1½ cups) beansprouts
- Juice 1 lemon
- ½ teaspoon sugar
- Red pepper flakes, to taste

Drain the tofu, cut it into bite-sized pieces and put it into a shallow dish with half the soy sauce. Leave to marinate for at least one hour, then gently cook in a dry frying pan, turning to seal each side.

Soak the noodles in cold water for 20 minutes. Drain.

Peel and finely chop the onion. Peel and chop the garlic. Roughly chop the peanuts.

Heat the oil in a wok and fry the onion and garlic for one minute, then stir in the tofu, noodles, beansprouts, peanuts, lemon juice, sugar, red pepper flakes and remaining soy sauce. Toss over a high heat for up to three minutes, until heated through.

Serves four.

17

TRY T'AI CHI

In China and other Eastern countries, elderly people can often be seen in the early morning practising the ancient art of t'ai chi in their local park. In so doing, they are not only promoting the smooth flow of their internal energy and therefore boosting their overall health, they are also doing their best to avoid an event responsible for more deaths to older people in the Western world than anything else – a fall.

To maximise your sense of balance and minimise the danger of falls, take a tip from the East and try a local t'ai chi class. Its slow, flowing movements are also likely to bring about an enhanced sense of inner calm.

18

DO GOOD DEEDS

Doing good deeds for others not only boosts your mood at the time but also leads to long-lasting happiness. Scientific studies show that acts of kindness have more of an impact on your wellbeing if you do a variety of different things rather than repeating the same activity on a number of occasions.

Researchers have suggested reasons why performing acts of kindness for others increases happiness. These include feeling more confident, in control and optimistic about your ability to make a difference; for instance, volunteering enables you to connect with other people and may help you feel more positive about the community in which you live.

19

SHARE THE DRIVING

Carpooling is a growing trend, and yet only a small minority of commuters make use of carpools. In many areas 80 per cent of people still drive to work alone when sharing a ride with someone just two days a week could reduce their carbon emissions by 725 kilograms (1,600 pounds) a year.

If you're looking for a ride or have one to share, there are great websites for connecting passengers and cars across the world. They connect commuters and cars according to where they live and where they are going, with data tailored to your specific area. Consider carpooling with other parents to get your children to school. With a little organisation carpooling can save time as well as help save our quickly warming planet. You can find out more about your local carshare opportunities at www.carpooling.co.uk.

20

WONDER AT THE WORLD

The ability to appreciate excellence is considered by philosophers to be a measure of perception and sensitivity, making it one of humanity's most important strengths. People who have a highly developed sense of what constitutes excellence feel a sense of wonderment at the natural world. They also have great respect for the gifts and talents of others, admiring how a potter can turn a shapeless lump of clay into a beautiful work of art, for example.

So open your eyes and wonder at the world and people around you – doing so may enrich your experience and appreciation of life's gifts.

21

KEEP YOUR MIND ACTIVE

Acquiring knowledge prompts the brain to create new links between nerve cells – a direct antidote to ageing – so don't stop learning when you leave full-time education. If you keep your mind active as you get older, you are more likely to keep your body active too, fending off a host of other age-related conditions.

The following activities keep your brain alert and can help lower the risk of developing Alzheimer's disease:

- Information-processing activities, such as listening to the radio or visiting museums
- Solving sudoku puzzles, completing crosswords or reading thought-provoking books
- A simple change in routine, such as trying out a new recipe.

22

BE ROMANTIC

Romance is essential for keeping couples in touch with each other as loving, sensual human beings.

It isn't just a question of buying flowers and other gifts. It includes any kind or thoughtful act that you might do for or with your partner; for instance, remembering to buy a favourite food at the delicatessen, sending a text message in the middle of the day or snuggling up on the sofa to watch a film together. Romance is any activity that says, 'I am thinking about you'.

DAILY INSPIRATION

'Rules for Happiness:
something to do,
someone to love,
something to hope for.'

Immanuel Kant
German philosopher (1724–1804)

24

STRETCH: KNEE TIP

This stretch can help cure muscle tightness in and around the spine and make the spine more flexible and mobile.

- Lie on your back with your feet flat on the floor, knees bent and together. Position your arms flat on the floor, at an angle to your body. Contract your stomach and pelvic muscles.
- Very gently tip both knees to one side. Tip your knees as far as is comfortable for you – if you can, tip them until your knees are resting on the floor. Look away from your knees over the opposite hand.
- Hold this position for 15 seconds. Perform this move again, tipping your knees to the other side of your body.

25

AVOID COMPARISON

Being confident in yourself and your lifestyle is a positive step towards happiness. Frequent comparisons to others can be destructive to this. Everyone is different, and accepting that will help you feel secure about your own situation.

- Acknowledge that there will always be someone better off than you. Notice when you start to make upward comparisons and divert your attention elsewhere.
- Avoid situations that lead to comparison. For example, stop buying celebrity magazines and reading newspaper 'rich lists'.
- Put everything in perspective. Will whatever you are concerned about now matter in the long term?

EAT FEWER SATURATED FATS

A diet high in saturated fat can raise the level of LDL cholesterol – the 'bad cholesterol' – in the blood, increasing the risk of heart disease. Saturated fat is found mostly in butter, cheese and fatty meat products such as sausages. Most of us consume about 20 per cent more than the recommended daily maximum of fat, which is 30 grams (1 ounce) for an average man and 20 grams (0.7 ounces) for an average woman.

You can find 'good' unsaturated fats in fish such as salmon and trout and also in seeds, nuts, avocados and some plant oils. In some instances, these may even help to reduce 'bad' cholesterol slightly.

Check nutritional labels on packaged food. More than 5 grams (0.18 ounces) of saturates per 100 grams (3.5 ounces) is high; 1.5 grams (0.05 ounces) per 100 grams (3.5 ounces) is low.

To cut down on your saturated fat consumption:

- Use low-fat versions of dairy products.
- Choose lean meat and skinless poultry; remove visible fat and skin.
- Grill meat instead of frying it.
- Eat fewer pastries, cakes, biscuits and crisps.

27

START GARDENING

There is nothing quite like being outside and getting your hands dirty. Regular gardening helps to keep you healthy, reducing cholesterol levels and the risk of heart disease, while improving manual dexterity and coordination skills. Studies also show that gardening reduces stress and depression and boosts self-esteem, resulting in an improvement in psychological wellbeing.

Growing your own food in your garden will also shrink your carbon footprint as it eliminates the need for transport, processing and packaging – all of which are major contributors to global warming.

Even if you don't have a garden, there are special containers that are ideal for cultivating flowers, herbs and vegetables on a balcony, windowsill or indoors.

28

DUST AWAY THOSE MITES

Plagued by itchy eyes, sneezing and a runny nose that never seems to go away? You are probably one of the many sufferers of allergic rhinitis, which affects around one in five people. The condition is caused by airborne particles, in particular dust mite allergens, which can also trigger asthma.

Good ventilation is crucial to help minimise allergens:

- Open windows for at least a couple of hours a day, except during the peak pollen season if you are a hay-fever sufferer.
- Turn down your central heating by a few degrees (dust mites like warm conditions).

GET HITCHED

Having close and loving relationships and feeling secure and attached to other people are fundamental human needs, contributing not only to the development of emotionally well-balanced adults but also to the survival of the human race. But one of the most reliable findings from numerous relationship studies is that people who are married tend to be happier than those who are not.

This research does not prove that getting married will make you happy per se. It does, however, indicate that getting married increases an individual's happiness regardless of how happy he or she was before marriage. Even after many years, those people who initially responded to marriage with a big increase in happiness retained enough to be happier than they were when single.

30

TRAIN THE BRAIN: QUICK CONUNDRUM

The following people were at a family reunion:

one grandfather,
one grandmother,
two fathers,
two mothers,
four children,
three grandchildren,
two sisters,
one brother,
two daughters,
two sons,
one father-in-law,
one mother-in-law,
and one daughter-in-law.

What's the fewest number of people attending, and who were they?

Answer: Seven people were at the reunion: two girls and a boy, their parents and their father's parents.

31

GET CREATIVE

Close links exist between creativity and happiness. In one experiment, one group of people watched a short comedy while another group watched a neutral clip. Those who had watched the comedy – purposely designed to induce a positive mood – performed better at tasks that required them to solve problems creatively than those who had watched the neutral clip.

Among the therapeutic benefits of creative activity are enhanced focus, greater self-esteem, a sense of control over one's life and increased energy and contentment.

32

JUICE DAY: LEMON AID JUICE

This juice gives the liver a kick-start to cleanse your body. Your bowels will also appreciate the gentle nudge into action. Each glass contains vitamins A and C, selenium and zinc – nutrients that will help replace those lost through burning the candle at both ends and give you energy to start your day.

- ½ grapefruit
- 1 kiwi fruit
- ½ lemon
- Large slice pineapple
- 60g (½ cup) frozen cranberries
- 60g (½ cup) frozen raspberries

Juice the grapefruit, kiwi, lemon and pineapple. Then blend the juice with the frozen berries in a blender. Drink immediately.

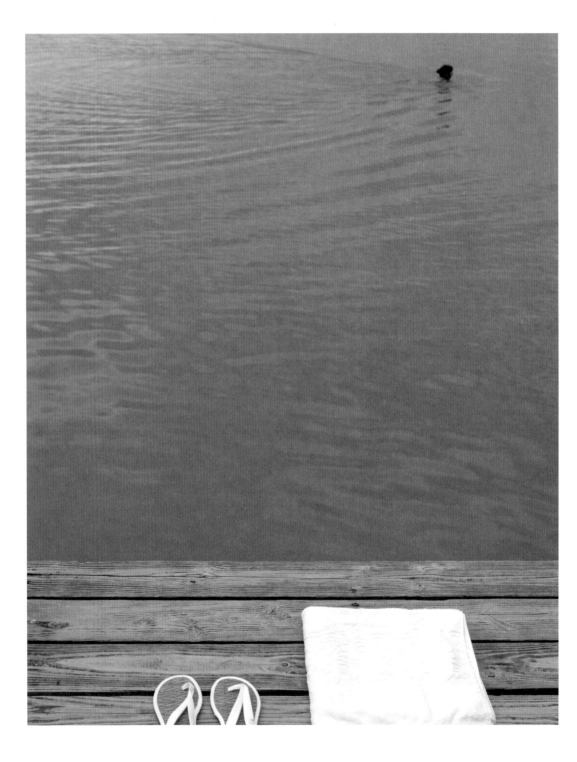

GO FOR A SWIM

Immersing yourself in a cool pool is a wonderful way to clear your mind and make you feel thoroughly refreshed, but there is a lot more to swimming than that. Whatever your age or ability and whichever stroke you prefer, swimming is excellent exercise for the whole body, improving strength, flexibility and balance, and offering a great cardiovascular workout.

As a low-impact exercise, swimming puts very little stress on the joints. This means that it is especially good for pregnant women and for people with chronic health problems such as arthritis or osteoporosis. It is also a useful aid to weight control. Swimming at a moderate pace can burn up to 300 calories in 30 minutes, as well as increasing energy levels and reducing stress. However, if you can't swim or dislike swimming, you might prefer to keep fit by joining an aqua aerobics class.

If you want to embark on a longer-term fitness plan, try this workout, which is designed to speed up your heart rate and tone your arms and thighs:

- Swim one length at your usual rate (overarm if possible), then one length as fast as you can.
- Alternate your speeds, as you'll work your body harder and get better results faster.
- Start with as many lengths as you can manage and aim to increase your workout by two lengths each week.

PRACTISE PILATES

Do you want to improve your posture and boost your core strength? Signing up for a Pilates class may be the answer.

Named after its founder Joseph Pilates, who developed the fitness programme during World War I, Pilates is a total body-conditioning workout that builds core strength, develops a graceful posture and creates a properly aligned body. Instead of concentrating on superficial muscles, it builds the deep muscles that protect the spine. Pilates also boosts the immune system, increases bone density, heals and prevents injuries and strains and makes your whole body more flexible.

Pilates can also improve mood and leave you feeling refreshed and revitalised. Pilates exercises release endorphins that promote a calm and happy state of mind. Also, like yoga, Pilates focuses your attention on breathing, which further enhances feelings of calm and concentration.

Here are some tips for beginning Pilates:

- Practise Pilates on an empty stomach and drink water beforehand so you do not dehydrate.
- Find a good teacher who will establish a correct routine and a regular class that will give you a solid basis for motivation.
- Start slowly and be realistic about how much you are prepared to do. Start with ten minutes of exercise between one and six times a week.
- Don't forget to breathe. Practise lateral breathing, which expands your ribcage sideways with every breath.
- Make sure you do different exercises to create a balanced sequence. Also, if you do an exercise that stretches one side of your body, always repeat the exercise on the other side.

35

STRETCH: THE SPHINX

The sphinx is a yoga position that focuses on the lower back. It gently stretches and lengthens the spine.

- Lie on your front and place your elbows and hands on the floor with your back slightly arched.
- Relax into this position and press your hips into the floor. This stretches the front abdominal muscles and you may feel some movement in your lower back. If you have no pain in this position you can move on to the next stage.
- Press on your hands and lift your elbows off the floor, arching your body further back. Hold this position for 15 seconds and then slowly release.

36

BE MINDFUL

Habits tend to occur unconsciously – we repeat them without thought because it's what we've always done. Yet when we turn our attention to our habitual behaviour and begin to establish habits more mindfully, we can vastly improve our sense of wellbeing.

You, not your habits, are in control of you, so take a few minutes to think about your existing habits and how they affect your mental, physical and spiritual health. Try listing your good and bad habits – give yourself credit for the good ones and then list some new habits that could replace bad ones.

MEDITATE

The psychological benefits of meditation are now recognised all over the world and it is even used in some hospitals to reduce stress associated with chronic or terminal illness. Studies of techniques such as transcendental meditation have shown that they can be effective in controlling blood pressure, keeping the arteries healthy and reducing the risk of heart disease.

Meditation can lift mood, dispel anxiety and be used to banish negative thoughts and pessimism. People who meditate regularly also say that it helps them to concentrate, improving their performance at work and bringing harmony to their relationships.

As well as reducing negative experiences such as stress, a sense of loneliness, negative body image and even chronic pain, meditation can also be used to enhance your resilience and ability to cope, aid relaxation, boost your energy and enthusiasm for life, improve your psychological wellbeing and happiness and heighten your awareness of subtle emotions.

Try this simple meditation exercise to get started:

- Sit or lie comfortably. If you are lying down, be careful not to fall asleep! Set a clock for the duration of the meditation, so you don't have to interrupt your peaceful thoughts to check the time.
- Close your eyes and begin breathing deeply. Allow your thoughts to release with each exhalation. Some people find it necessary to focus on a word or number so that their minds don't wander. If you prefer, use the simple method of counting. With each breath out, count one, with the next breath out, two, and so on. Over time your mind will wander, so when it does, just begin at one and start counting again.
- If you find it impossible to still your mind the moment your eyes close, try this method instead. Light a candle and stare into the centre of the flame. Blink whenever necessary and allow your breathing to be calm and steady.

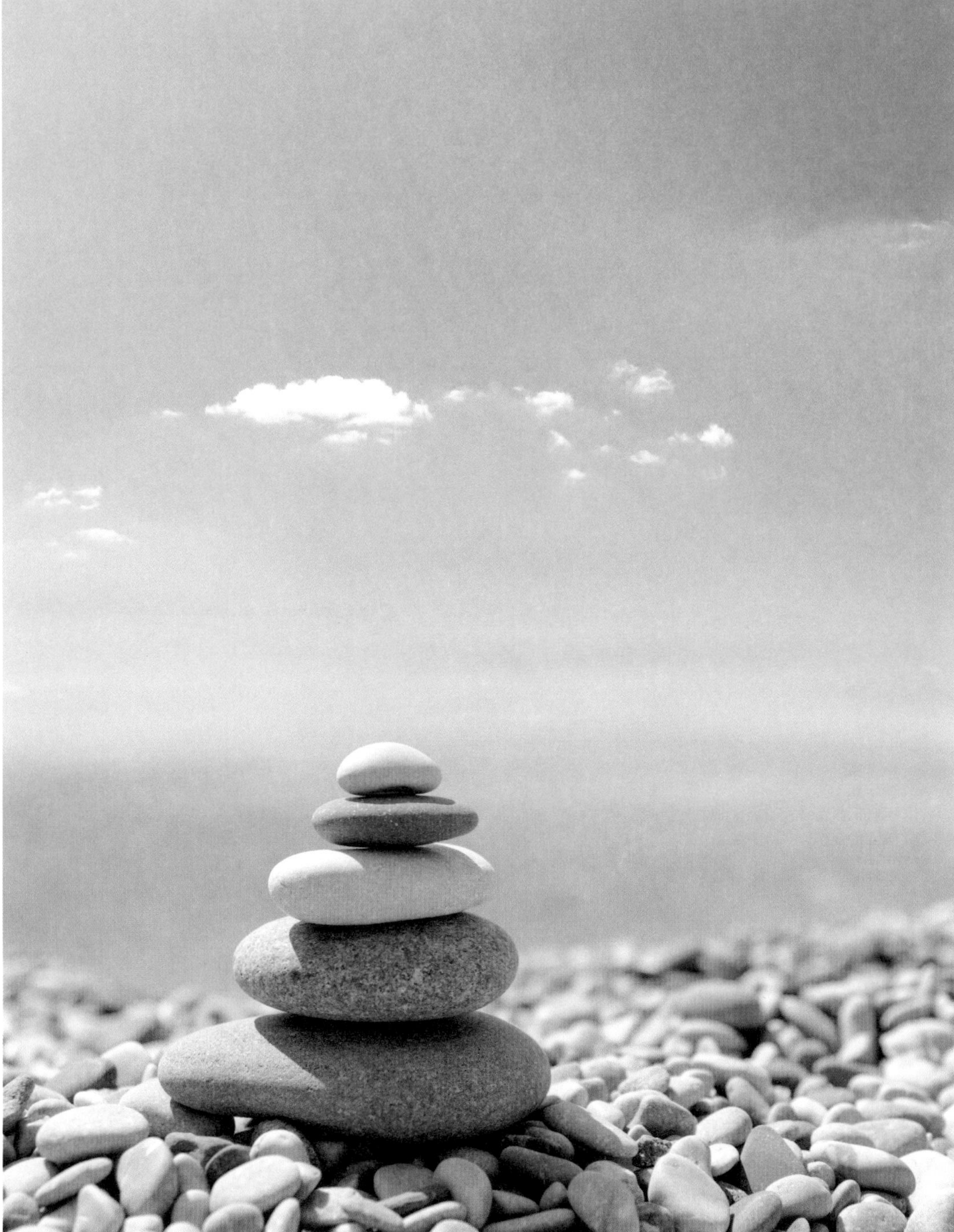

38

TRAIN THE BRAIN: WORD PLAY

This exercise tests your ability to select the correct word from a selection of words that are commonly confused.

1: I _____ down for a nap yesterday.

(a) lied (b) laid (c) lay

2: _____ book is this?

(a) Who's (b) Whose (c) Whom

3: _____________ went to the cinema yesterday.

(a) My friend and me (b) Me and my friend (c) My friend and I

Answers: 1. c, 2. b, 3. c

39

STAND TALL

Most of us decide what we think about other people within minutes of meeting them. Your posture, facial expressions, hand gestures and eye contact can reveal more than a thousand words.

The first rule for appearing confident and relaxed is to stand or sit with a straight back and a long neck. Look directly at the person you are talking to, keep your chin up and use plenty of eye contact. Smiling often and nodding occasionally indicates that you are focused and interested in the conversation.

Actions such as running your fingers through your hair and laughing a lot can be interpreted as flirtatious, so take care not to send out the wrong signals.

40

DISCOVER THE POWER OF SCENT

Whether it's the smell of freshly mown grass or freshly brewed coffee, scents can have an effect on your mood, personal relationships and sense of wellbeing.

The part of the brain that processes smell interacts with the areas that store memories, meaning that particular smells can produce very powerful emotional reactions. But beyond memory and personal association, certain more 'universal' scents can have a positive effect on your physical wellbeing and emotional state. For instance, citrusy scents like lemon and grapefruit are known to energise your mind, while many floral scents like jasmine, lavender and chamomile produce calm.

Research also suggests that our attraction to someone may be based on the pheromones (airborne chemical triggers) that they release – in other words, scent may even influence who we are attracted to and when we are most attracted to them.

There are many ways to introduce vibrant or relaxing scents into your home. A bunch of scented flowers, such as freesias, jasmine, lilies, roses or scented geraniums, can make a real difference to the smell of a room and bring you closer to nature. Try using essential oils or purchase an organic aromatherapy candle. Even finding a perfume that you love and you feel expresses your personality is important as it can lift your mood and self-confidence.

RELAX AND UNWIND: GOLDEN THREAD BREATH

This breathing technique involves using a visualisation to promote a sense of calm in both the body and mind. It is invaluable any time you feel a little stressed or overwhelmed by life's ups and downs.

- Sit in a comfortable upright position and breathe naturally, in through your nose and out through slightly parted lips.
- As you exhale, imagine you are slowly and carefully blowing a fine golden thread out of your mouth, relaxing deeply as you do so. As you gently inhale, feel the oxygen fill your lungs and vital energy fill your body.
- As you exhale, imagine the breath – and thread – gradually getting longer, moving further away from you, until it can reach no further. Then once again slowly and gently breathe in.
- Enjoy crafting the imaginary golden thread on each out-breath and replenishing your energy on each in-breath, creating a sense of calming and healing energy as you go.
- Continue with this technique until you feel suitably relaxed.

42

EAT OMEGA-3S

A group of polyunsaturated fatty acids called omega-3s are essential for healthy growth and development. They prevent coronary heart disease, high blood pressure, diabetes and arthritis, among a host of other conditions.

Oily fish is an excellent source of omega-3s. Aim to eat at least two portions a week of mackerel, salmon or sardines. Replace refined vegetable oils with flaxseed, walnut and rapeseed oils, which are richer in alpha-linolenic acid, a type of omega-3. Seek medical advice about taking supplements.

43

DO A COOL WASH

Washing clothes at low temperatures is the most effective way to reduce carbon dioxide emissions while doing the laundry. If everybody in a country simply washed at 30° Celsius (85° Fahrenheit) rather than 40° Celsius (100° Fahrenheit), the total energy savings could be over a billion kilowatt-hours of electricity per year.

There are other ways to increase the efficiency and lower the carbon emissions of your washing machine: use concentrated products, make sure that you are using the right amount of product for each wash, and only do a wash when you have a full load of laundry.

BE OPTIMISTIC

Do you look on the bright side of life rather than worrying about the what-might-have-beens? If so, this is good news for both your mental and physical wellbeing. Research has shown that optimistic people experience less distress, anxiety and depression than pessimists. Optimists learn from negative events and persevere with difficult tasks, assuming that solutions can be found.

But optimists don't necessarily see the world through rose-tinted spectacles. They heed health warnings and take action, rather than sticking their heads in the sand. They eat better and have more regular medical check-ups.

Here are some tips for looking at life more optimistically:

- Learn to recognise and put aside negative forms of thinking.
- Avoid filtering (focusing only on negative things) and personalising (blaming yourself for bad things).
- Work hard at taking a more positive view of life.
- Look for the good things, no matter how small, and cherish them.
- Try to play down the bad things – deal with them and move on.
- Keep company with optimists and hope their attitude rubs off on you.

45

DRINK MORE WATER

Water accounts for almost two-thirds of our body weight and is needed for every chemical reaction in our cells. It plays a vital role in metabolism, helping to absorb and transport nutrients and to flush out waste products. Even minor dehydration can affect physical, mental and emotional wellbeing. Our bodies lose water constantly through breathing, sweating and passing urine, and we need to replace this to stay healthy. The total amount of water lost daily is about 2.5 litres (5.5 pints), but we get 1 litre (2 pints) of the fluid we need from food and the body recovers 0.3 litres (10 fluid ounces) through chemical processes. The rest must come from drinks. All non-alcoholic drinks count, but water, milk and unsweetened fruit juices are the healthiest. To prevent dehydration, we should drink about 1.2 litres (2.5 pints) of fluid every day (equivalent to six 200-millilitre (3.75-fluid-ounce) glasses).

46

BANISH YOUR CARES WITH CHAMOMILE

The chamomile plant can be used to improve your wellbeing in a few different ways. The volatile oils in chamomile contain antibacterial compounds that help to soothe skin inflammation and promote healing. Chamomile tea is renowned for its ability to calm the nerves and promote sound sleep, making it a popular remedy for insomnia. The tea also has a relaxing, anti-inflammatory effect on the digestive tract, helping to relieve indigestion and diverticular disorders.

DAILY INSPIRATION

‘One of the lessons that I grew up with was to always stay true to yourself and never let what somebody else says distract you from your goals.’

Michelle Obama
First Lady of the United States (1964–)

HEALTH DAY:
SPRING VEGETABLES WITH RED PESTO

'Baby' or 'new' vegetables are either cultivated miniature vegetables or vegetables that have been picked before full maturity. Nevertheless, they contain just as many nutrients as their full-sized counterparts. Spring is the perfect time to embrace these tender and tasty miniatures.

- 225g (½ lb) new potatoes
- 225g (½ lb) baby carrots
- 175g (6 oz) baby courgettes
- 8 shallots
- 85g (3 oz) baby asparagus spears
- 85g (3 oz) fine green beans

For the pesto:

- 2 tomatoes
- Handful fresh basil
- 2 cloves garlic
- 55g (2 oz) Parmesan cheese
- 1 tablespoon olive oil

Bring a pan of salted water to the boil and cook the potatoes for up to 15 minutes, until tender. Trim the remaining vegetables and chop into bite-sized pieces, then steam them for 10 minutes, until tender.

To make the pesto, roughly chop the tomatoes and basil. Peel and crush the garlic, and grate the cheese. Put all the ingredients into a food processor, and process to a rough paste.

Toss the cooked vegetables with the pesto and serve immediately.

Serves four.

49

GET A GLOW

Steaming your skin not only gives it a healthy glow but also helps to unblock pores. Use this treatment once a week. Red clover leaves are available from herbalists and some pharmacists.

1 tablespoon dried lavender

50g (¼ cup) fresh strawberries

1 tablespoon red clover leaves

Sprinkle the lavender, strawberries and red clover leaves into a bowl of steaming water. Place your face over the steamy mixture and cover your head with a towel. Stay in position for 5–15 minutes. Rinse your face with cool water and pat dry.

50

EAT LOCAL

On average, fresh produce travels around 2,415 kilometres (1,500 miles) from source to plate. Reduce that figure by eating locally sourced food. Choosing to eat from the earth around you also supports local, independent farmers, many of whom strive to grow their produce in a sustainable way. At the same time, the processing, packaging and fuel costs to the environment are virtually eliminated.

51

BALANCE LIFE AND WORK

Research suggests that people who focus on meaningful relationships are more satisfied with life and less prone to depression than those who seek wealth and material success above all else. This helps to explain how stress and work/life balance have become such important topics in Western cultures: people find conflict between their obligations (such as working long hours) and their underlying values (such as prioritising family).

A way to deal with this conflict could be to dedicate time specifically to both causes. Knowing that you have set aside definite time will help you feel in control and you won't feel like you are being pulled in two opposing directions.

52

TRY GINKGO BILOBA

The beautiful fan-shaped leaves of the ginkgo biloba tree are the source of one of the world's most popular herbal remedies. Many people believe their concentrated extract, taken as a supplement, can boost memory and concentration. In one study of healthy volunteers, researchers reported a sustained improvement in attention from the consumption of ginkgo supplements.

So try some ginkgo for yourself and see if your brain power improves. Ginkgo extract can be obtained from many health food stores. Often bought as a dietary supplement, it can take the form of tablets, capsules or liquids.

SEVEN NUTRIENTS THAT MATTER

The right combination of vitamins and minerals is crucial to all-round wellbeing. A balanced diet that draws on all the main food types – fruit and vegetables, starchy carbohydrates, milk and dairy products, meat, fish and eggs, fats and sugars – should naturally provide the essential vitamins and minerals that you need. Here is a quick checklist of seven of the most essential vitamins and minerals:

Folic acid: (from broccoli, asparagus and peas). Deficiency causes fatigue, confusion and irritability.

Vitamin B12: (from meat, salmon, milk, eggs and yeast extract). Severe deficiency results in loss of memory, mental dysfunction and depression.

Vitamin C: (from peppers, broccoli, oranges and kiwi fruit). High-dose vitamin C supplements have been shown to reduce depression.

Selenium: (from brazil nuts, bread, fish, meat and eggs). Individuals given daily selenium supplements for five or six weeks showed distinctly improved moods.

Iron: (from liver, dried fruit, wholegrains and green leafy vegetables). Deficiency leads to fatigue, irritability, apathy and inability to concentrate.

Zinc: (from meat, shellfish, dairy foods and cereal products). Deficiency may lead to depression.

Omega-3: (from fatty fish, organic free-range eggs, nuts and seeds, and brown rice). Deficiency may lead to increased incidences of depression and anxiety.

54

LEARN FLOWER ARRANGING

Having stunning displays of fresh flowers around your home can help to give a sense of warmth and vibrancy to your living space. And arranging them yourself will create an even greater feel-good factor. Here are some tips for effective flower arranging:

- Choose a combination of long, straight stems, 'rounded' flowers and leaves, and 'filler' material, to fill any unwanted gaps.
- Always cut stems at an angle before placing them in the water, and trim off any leaves below the water's surface.
- Allow some space between flowers to prevent overcrowding.
- When using open flowers, such as daffodils and gerbera, turn them to face different directions for heightened interest.

55

PLANT A TREE

Trees offer many benefits – not least of which is their calming effect. According to a study at Texas A & M University, looking at a leafy landscape for just five minutes can reduce blood pressure and ease muscle tension.

Planting a tree will provide you with shade in summer and act as a windbreak in winter – and it can make a small but significant difference to an individual's carbon footprint. One acre of forest absorbs six tonnes of carbon dioxide and releases four tonnes of oxygen into the atmosphere each year. A campaign launched by the United Nations in 2006 in recognition of this fact has already resulted in the planting of 12.5 billion trees.

56

MONITOR YOUR BMI

Being overweight is intrinsically linked to a heightened risk of heart attack, stroke, cancer, diabetes and joint disease. A study conducted in 2006 collated data from more than half a million Americans and found that even small increases in body mass index (BMI) can lead to premature death.

To discover your BMI, measure and write down your height in metres, square the figure, and then divide your weight in kilograms by your squared height. A normal BMI is between 18.5 and 25. A BMI above 30 indicates obesity. Bear in mind, however, that this is only one indicator of your overall health, and that muscle weighs more than fat.

57

MAKE NEW FRIENDS

One of the keys to staying mentally alert as we grow older is to continue to take an interest in other people – and it's never too late to make new friends. Indeed, close friendships can have a positive bearing on all aspects of our lives, from our careers to the way we bring up our children. Studies have shown that people who have fulfilling relationships suffer less stress, recover more quickly from illness and live longer. An important aspect of making new friends is to take the initiative. If you meet someone you'd like to see again, get in touch and make an arrangement. Don't wait for him or her to contact you. And get involved with activity groups so you keep meeting new people.

58

TRUST YOURSELF

How often have you gone along with something because you've been told that others do it too? It can sometimes encourage good behaviour, but submission to authority at the expense of independent thought also leads to bad choices. The Milgram experiment is a famous case at Yale University – volunteers were instructed by an authority to give electric shocks to subjects behind a screen. Remarkably, the volunteers continued to obey, responding with herd mentality and ignoring their own conscience.

If you doubt what someone does or says, trust your instincts rather than be influenced. Have confidence in your knowledge and beliefs and don't assume others are right on the basis that they seem authoritative or are 'in charge'. Try to imagine how you would act if you were bearing sole responsibility.

59

EAT AN APPLE A DAY

We all know the saying 'an apple a day keeps the doctor away' and there really does seem to be some truth in it. As well as containing vitamin C and fibre, apples have a laxative effect on your body due to their pectin content, which encourages excretion of certain metals. This is ideal if you've been overindulging on crisps and sweets, as pectin also helps to remove food additives from the system. So next time you're feeling sluggish and in need of a mini detox, be sure to fill your shopping basket with some juicy apples.

USE ESSENTIAL OILS

Essential oils are a wonderful way to bring the healing benefits of aromatherapy into your life. They are versatile too: you can add them to a hot bath, use them to scent pot pourri, burn them in oil burners or mix them in massage oils. Find essential oils at your local herbalist or pharmacy.

Essential oils have surprising health benefits that can relieve everything from insomnia to skin problems. Here is a short list of oils and their benefits:

Lavender: Known for curing insomnia and its ability to soothe frayed nerves. It can also be used to treat cuts and skin irritation.

May Chang: Good for increasing energy, lifting mood and beating depression.

Calendula: Can be used to reduce the appearance of acne and scars and is particularly good for sensitive skin.

Oregano: Has potent anitbacterial properties which make it an effective fighter against colds and other sicknesses.

Grapefruit: Great for boosting alertness and minimising fatigue. Grapefruit oil can also be used in natural homemade cleaning products because of its antiseptic qualities.

Eucalyptus: Good for fighting colds, relieving breathing problems and stimulating the immune system. Only use it diluted, as undiluted it can irritate your skin.

61

WELCOME NEW CHALLENGES

Taking on new challenges, learning new skills and developing interests in new directions can make a real difference to your happiness. Studies show that people who set goals that are designed to fulfil their potential as individuals are likely to experience greater life satisfaction and less depression.

According to American psychologist Carol Ryff, people who score highly in personal initiative assessments exhibit the following characteristics:

- They are open to unfamiliar experiences and activities.
- They think it is important to have experiences that challenge the way they view themselves and the world.
- They are stimulated by the idea of continual intellectual growth.

62

MAKE PLASTIC BAGS HISTORY

Between 500 billion and 1 trillion plastic bags are distributed worldwide each year and less than three per cent are recycled. Most end up in landfills, where they can take a thousand years to biodegrade. Others find their way to the oceans, where they suffocate aquatic life, or into the countryside, where they deface the natural environment and can be eaten by grazing animals.

Make a difference; take a basket or a cloth bag with you every time you go shopping, and reuse the old plastic bags that you have lying around.

HEALTH DAY: ASPARAGUS TAGLIATELLE

Asparagus contains an amino acid called asparagine, which, along with its high potassium content and low sodium, makes it a diuretic and a cleanser, useful for processing proteins and flushing through the kidneys. Diuretics help reduce both blood pressure and water retention in the legs.

- 450g (1 lb) asparagus
- 400g (14 oz) fresh tagliatelle
- Small handful fresh, flat-leaf parsley
- Few sprigs fresh dill
- Few sprigs fresh chives
- 3 tablespoons lemon oil
- 1 tablespoon sea salt flakes

Cut the asparagus into short pieces – using just the tips is prettiest for this dish, but you can use the stems too, or reserve them for another dish. Prepare a large saucepan of boiling salted water, with a steamer on top. Cook the pasta in the water, and at the same time, steam the asparagus tips. Both the pasta and the asparagus tips should be ready in around five minutes. While cooking, chop the herbs.

Drain the pasta and arrange it on four serving plates, topped with the asparagus, chopped herbs, lemon oil and a sprinkle of sea salt flakes, to taste.

Serves four.

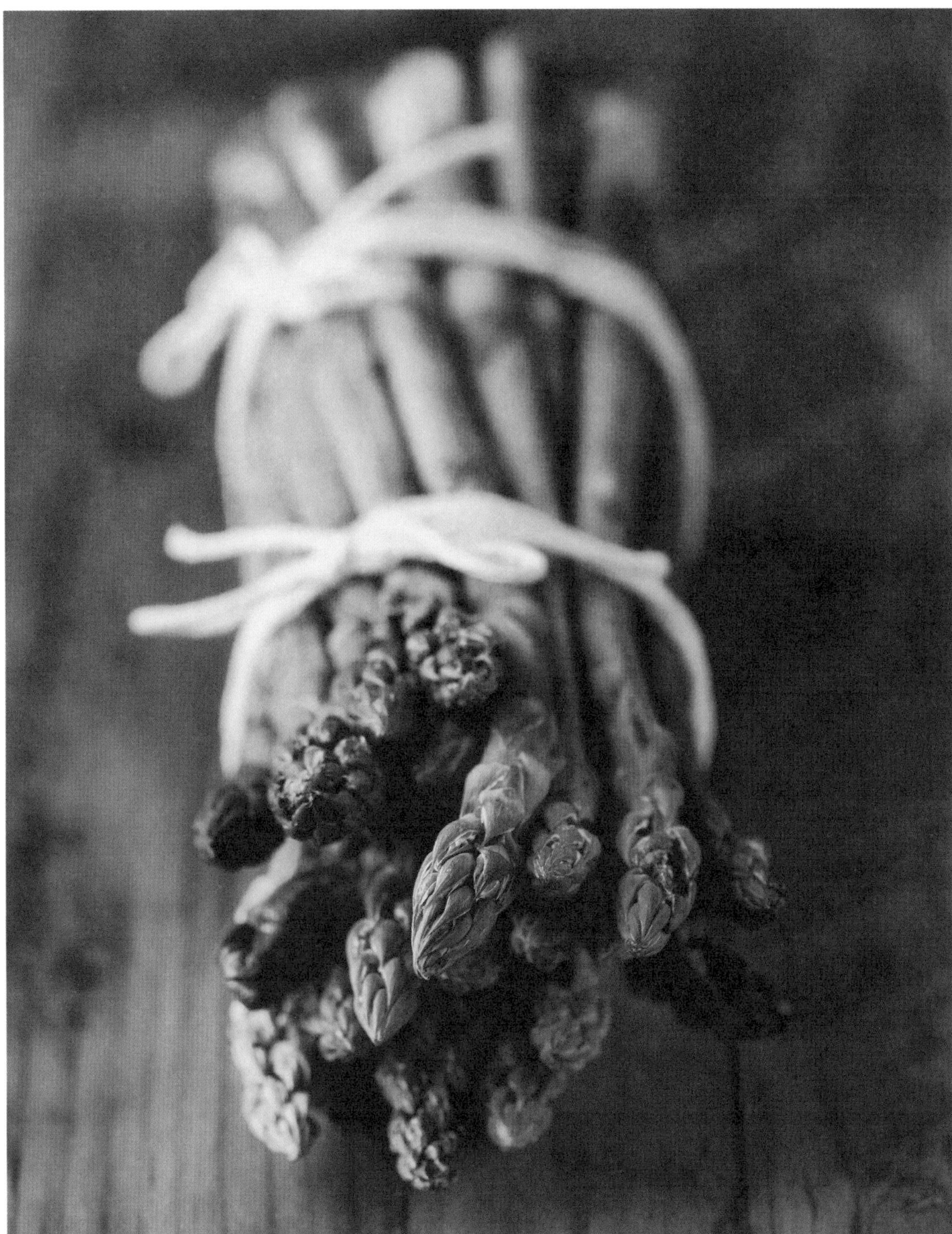

LIMIT DAMAGE FROM FREE RADICALS

Our bodies are under constant attack at a sub-microscopic level from free radicals – unstable atoms that react with nearby compounds to regain stability – which exist in our bodies and in the environment. The cells of the immune system generate free radicals, for example, to neutralise invading viruses and bacteria. But free radicals can also damage a cell's own components, such as genetic material or proteins. This is a contributory factor in the ageing process, as well as in illnesses such as cancer and cardiovascular disease.

Environmental hazards increase our exposure to free radicals. But they may also enter the body in food or directly through the skin. Once in the body, they may trigger a sequence of activation of enzymes, inflammation and release of chemical signals, which harms the tissues. The body uses antioxidants – molecules that safely react with free radicals – to limit the damage. But as we get older our antioxidant processes become less efficient, so we need to take in extra antioxidant nutrients, and reduce environmental exposure. Here are some simple steps you can take:

- Avoid traffic exhaust fumes, which are high in cadmium.
- Steer clear of cigarette smoke.
- Reduce exposure to synthetic chemicals such as insecticides.
- Avoid exposure to heavy metals such as mercury, cadmium and lead.
- Avoid ionizing radiation from industrial pollution, sun exposure and medical X-rays.

65

AVOID FAD DIETS

It can be all too easy to be lured in by the latest crash diet, often endorsed by pictures of celebrities and attention-grabbing headlines. These diets are usually lauded as flawless weight-loss regimes, but that couldn't be further from the truth. Losing weight too quickly is very harmful to your health, depriving you of essential nutrients and disrupting how your body functions. Such short-term methods can also be miserable to undertake and, in the long term, can leave you worse off than when you started.

The guide to achieving and maintaining a healthy weight is to exercise regularly and eat well. Keep your diet varied and balanced and there will be no need for drastic weight-loss measures. Your body will be healthy, you won't be cutting out essential food types and you'll be happier as a result. Slow and steady wins the race!

66

FEED THE BRAIN

The brain is a special organ: it requires a lot of metabolic energy and its cells are particularly long-lived. Unfortunately, these characteristics leave the brain's tissue vulnerable to damage from free radicals – chemicals that react easily with other molecules. Fortunately, many vegetables are high in antioxidants, molecules that counteract the damage done by free radicals – so make sure you get plenty in your diet. Antioxidants can be found in:

- Leafy green vegetables, such as spinach, lettuce and chard
- Cruciferous vegetables, such as broccoli and cauliflower
- Bright peppers, such as sweet peppers and chilli peppers.

DAILY INSPIRATION

'One cannot live well, love well, sleep well, if one does not eat well.'

Virginia Woolf
English author (1882–1941)

68

GIVE UP SMOKING

Cigarette smoking is the single most important cause of preventable disease and premature death in developed countries. The good news is, once you give up smoking, your health risks rapidly drop. Here are some tips to help you on your way to stopping:

- Quit when you are in the right frame of mind. Believe that you will be successful.
- Follow a structured plan, taking it one day at a time.
- Use medical treatments such nicotine-replacement therapy or anti-craving drugs as advised by a health professional.
- If your attempt to stop fails, don't give up. Make a mental note of what factors did or didn't work for you so that next time you will be successful.

69

MAKE A WILL

We often put off making a will, but it is a gift we can give our family and friends that really can mean a great deal. People who die intestate can cause a multitude of problems for the loved ones left behind.

In the absence of a will, the state will decide who inherits – so your friends, relatives and favoured charities may get nothing. It is particularly important to make a will if you are not married or in a registered civil partnership. Otherwise, even if you have lived together for many years, your cohabitant may be left with nothing.

PLANT FOR THE PLANET

If you care about the environment, conserve water by choosing to cultivate plants that are well adapted to the natural climate and require minimal maintenance. Wildflower gardens are a desirable substitute for a well-mown grassy lawn since they consist mainly of either indigenous species or plants that are suited to local weather conditions. Verdant plants and delicate flowers such as juniper, nasturtium, sage, thyme, lavender and evening primrose are suitable for a dry, sunny environment. For damper soils, choose columbine, meadowsweet, hemp agrimony, sneezewort and teasels. Devil's-bit scabious also thrives in damp conditions, and is a great late-summer nectar source for bumblebees and butterflies.

EAT HERBS FOR HEALTH

Cultivating herbs for culinary and aesthetic reasons is a popular activity, but it can also benefit your health, since many herbs are packed full of nutrients.

Basil: Smelling a few basil leaves can help to relieve a tension or migraine headache and soothe menstrual symptoms. Consuming basil can ease bloating and stomach cramps.

Bay leaves: These contain laurenolide, an energising ingredient, making them useful in a long-term detox programme.

Coriander seed: This is used as an antibacterial treatment and to alleviate colic, neuralgia and rheumatism.

Dandelion: This contains potassium, a diuretic, which extracts salt and water from the kidneys so it is useful for anyone suffering from water retention.

Sage: Long considered a panacea for many health issues, sage is anti-inflammatory, antimicrobial and is a good source of antioxidants.

Thyme: Thyme is loaded with antioxidants, including thymol, which has been shown to increase the number of healthy fats in cell structures. Thyme also helps to effectively relieve and treat nose and throat illnesses as well as digestive issues.

Mint: Cooling, calming and refreshing, mint eases stomach and digestive problems, relaxes the mind and relieves headaches.

Parsley: Packed full of vitamin C, parsley is a natural breath freshener. It also contains flavonoids, such as luteolin; these are powerful antioxidants that neutralise the free radicals produced by pollution, helping to prevent cell damage.

72

TAKE CONTROL

Psychologists such as Daniel Nettle have argued that, rather than money, it is the sense of control over one's own life that is the largest contributory factor to wellbeing, life satisfaction and health. The more you feel that you can direct the course of your life and manage your work, family and relationships successfully, the happier and healthier you are likely to be. Here are ways to start taking charge of your life:

- Solidify your goals and formulate how you can realistically achieve them.
- If your expenses are getting out of control, target your spending weaknesses, create a budget and stick to it.
- Make a to-do list every day to map out your day. Check the items off as you complete them to feel a sense of satisfaction.

73

STRETCH: SIDE STRETCH

This stretch is good for your arms and upper body – it can also help loosen and tone the torso. When you've practised the stretch on one side, remember to repeat on the other side.

- Stand with your legs wide apart. Bend one leg and lean towards the bent leg. Make sure the bent knee is directly over the supporting foot.
- Reach the arm on the opposite side to the bent leg straight up and then lean your whole body into the stretch. Hold for a few seconds.

74

BE GI-WISE

The rate at which carbohydrates in foods are broken down and released into the bloodstream as glucose is reflected in the glycaemic index (GI). Foods that are low on the index release their energy slowly and steadily, helping to stabilise blood-sugar levels. High-GI foods, such as bread made from refined white flour, break down quickly and cause a rapid rise in blood sugar. This is followed by an equally rapid drop that will leave you feeling tired, lethargic and craving a 'sugar boost'.

People who change to a low-GI diet see many health benefits, including an increase in energy, cognitive performance and a reduction in the number of calories consumed. Eating regular meals will also help to sustain your blood glucose at a steady level.

Foods with a low GI include:

- Porridge and natural muesli
- Multi-grain bread
- Wholewheat pasta, beans and lentils
- Low-fat milk and yoghurt
- Most fruit
- Salad with a vinaigrette dressing
- Sweet potatoes.

75

BE BREAST AWARE

Staying alert for early signs of breast cancer could mean the difference between life and death. The earlier a tumour is spotted the easier it may be to treat. Cancer may appear between breast scans or before the first scan, so it's worth checking yourself regularly. A woman's breasts can look and feel different at different points in the menstrual cycle and at different ages. But be wary of any changes and talk to your doctor if you notice the following:

- Changes in the shape of the breast or the position of the nipple or the direction it points in, especially if the nipple inverts
- Different sensations in the breast or the skin over it, including pain, heaviness or numbness
- Dimpling, puckering or unusual thickening of the skin as well as changes to the nipple such as itching, discharge or bleeding.

76

TRAIN THE BRAIN: NUMBER TEASERS

Fine-tune your left-brained thinking by answering as many of the following questions as you can in three minutes:

a: What is the missing number? 1, 4, 9, ?, 25

b: If pears are priced at five for 75p how many can you buy for £2.85 (assuming they can also be bought individually)?

c: What number is $\frac{1}{4}$ of $\frac{1}{2}$ of $\frac{1}{2}$ of 400?

Answers: a. 16, b. 19, c. 25

77

READ

Here are some great reasons why you should become a regular reader:

Relaxation and escapism: Delving into a fiction book is a great way to remove yourself from everyday life.

Increased vocabulary and writing skills: You are exposed to new words naturally and can see them in context. Also, reading the well-crafted words of an experienced author can show you various ways of writing and improve your skills.

Cognitive stimulation: Reading 'exercises' your brain and keeping an active mind has been shown to lower the risk of developing Alzheimer's.

Memory improvement: Remembering complex storylines, sub-plots and various characters exercises your memory.

78

CUT DOWN ON SUGAR

Cakes, biscuits and fizzy drinks are full of sucrose, and even some 'savoury' processed foods contain more sugar than ice cream. Eating a high-sugar diet can cause tooth decay and excessive weight gain, which can lead to heart disease and type-2 diabetes.

The British Dietetic Association recommends that 'added sugars', including those in soft drinks and processed food, should not exceed 10 per cent of total daily calorie intake. For someone consuming 2,000 calories a day, that would amount to 50 grams (1.75 ounces) – the amount of sugar in a half-litre bottle of cola. So it's good to keep a close eye on the amount of sweet and processed food and drink that you consume.

79

INCREASE YOUR FIBRE INTAKE

Soluble fibre slows down the absorption of carbohydrates into the blood, helping to keep blood-sugar level constant. The recommended intake of fibre for adults is 18 grams (0.63 ounces) a day, but the average intake is only about 13 grams (0.45 ounces) for women and 15 grams (0.5 ounces) for men, meaning many people don't have enough fibre in their diet. Just one slice of wholemeal bread would add 4 grams (0.14 ounces) to your fibre intake, while a medium-sized baked potato with skin would add 5 grams (0.17 ounces). Some good sources of fibre are:

- Wholegrain foods, including bread and pasta
- Certain fruits, including avocados, berries, plums, bananas
- Certain vegetables, including broccoli, cauliflower, carrots
- Pulses (beans, chickpeas and lentils).

80

COMPOST

Composting organic waste has the dual benefit of reducing the rubbish in your dustbin and yielding good-quality homemade fertilizer. A household that discards one bin's worth of waste every week generates about 1,400 kilograms (3,086 pounds) of carbon dioxide a year – a figure that could be cut by 20 per cent if all kitchen and garden waste were composted.

When organic waste breaks down in landfill sites, it also produces methane, a gas with 21 times as much 'global-warming potential' as carbon dioxide. If you compost all your food waste, you can save about 5 kilograms (11 pounds) of methane emissions annually from being generated.

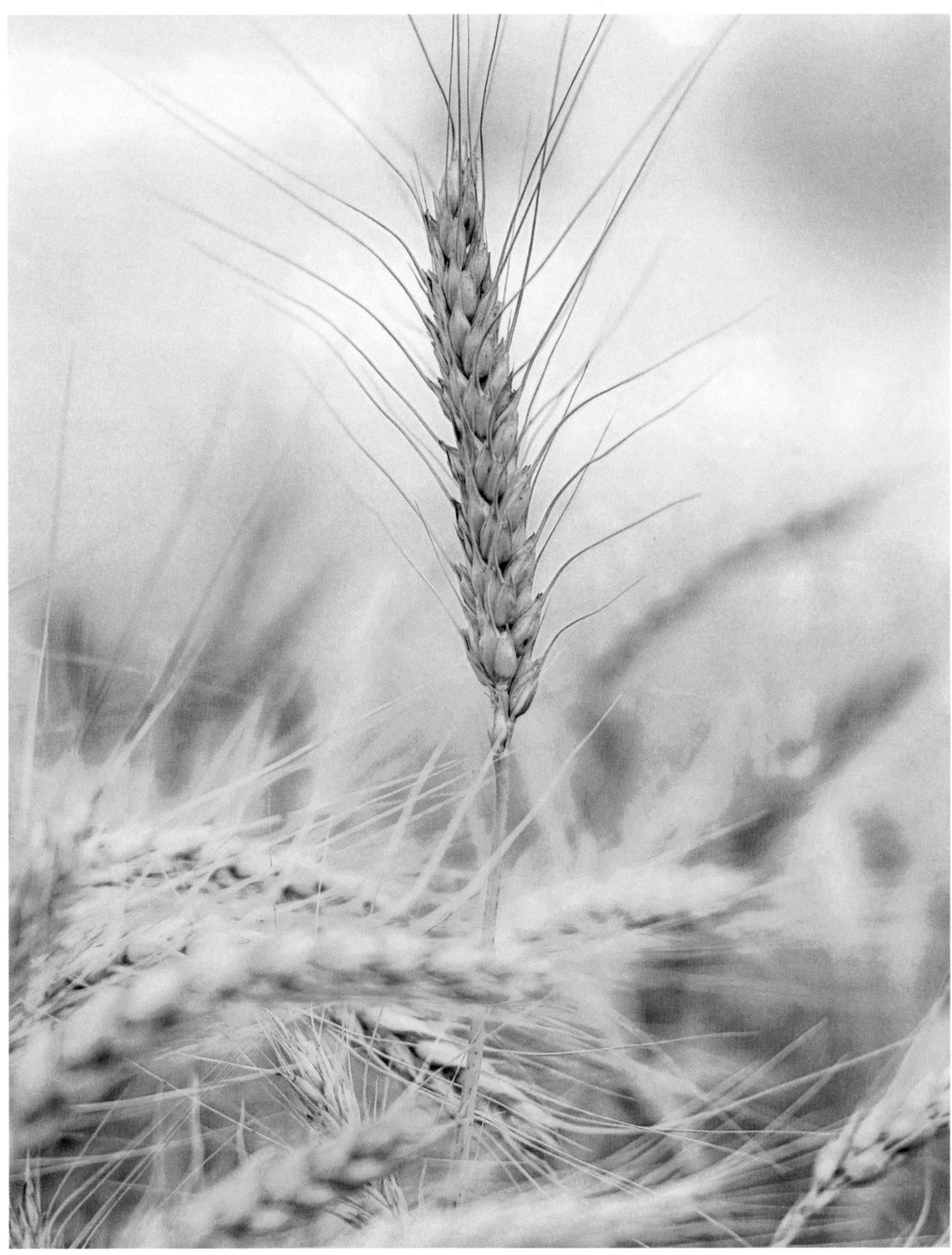

81

DON'T LINGER AT WORK

Researchers have found that long working hours are linked to poor sleep and serious health problems, including diabetes. One study showed that people who regularly worked three or more hours of overtime a day ran a higher risk of developing cardiovascular disease than those who worked contractual hours.

In another study of public servants, those who worked more than 55 hours a week were found to suffer a long-term decline in their mental acuity compared with those who stopped after 40 hours a week. At the end of the study, the lingerers had noticeably lower scores in tests that measured memory, attention and speed of information processing. The bottom line seems to be that even if you work overtime, you may not be spending that time effectively. So, isn't it time you went home?

82

BE DECISIVE

What happens to us in life depends on a multitude of personal decisions, small and large, but all too often we cannot make up our minds about the best course of action.

To reduce the amount of time you spend dithering, start by convincing yourself that you are decisive. Imagine yourself as the sort of person who can make quick and firm choices, and don't be afraid to make mistakes. There are no inherently 'good' or 'bad' decisions – just ones that will take you in different directions. Listen to your instincts and learn from experience, but don't dwell on analysing what might have gone wrong. It may help to give yourself deadlines.

HEALTH DAY: RHUBARB, PECAN AND GOAT'S CHEESE SALAD

Rhubarb is a spring vegetable known for its fleshy, edible stalks. Rhubarb is low in calories and rich in vitamin K, which helps blood to clot, builds strong bones and, as recently discovered, strengthens cognitive function.

3 sticks rhubarb
2 tablespoons agave syrup
55g (½ cup) pecans
175g (2 cups) mixed salad
55g (1 cup) goat's cheese

For the dressing:

1 shallot
2 tablespoons balsamic vinegar
1 tablespoon rapeseed oil
Salt and freshly ground black pepper

Preheat the oven to 230°C. Trim the rhubarb and cut into 1cm (½in) chunks. Place in a mixing bowl and toss in the agave syrup. Transfer to a baking tray lined with parchment paper and bake for five minutes, until the rhubarb starts to soften. Roughly chop the pecans. Toast them in a dry frying pan for a few minutes, until aromatic.

To make the dressing, peel the shallot and chop it very finely. Beat the shallot in with the remaining dressing ingredients.

Toss the rhubarb, mixed salad, pecans, goat's cheese and dressing in a bowl. Serve immediately.

Serves four.

DAILY INSPIRATION

'If you want others to be happy,
practise compassion.
If you want to be happy,
practise compassion.'

Dalai Lama
Spiritual leader of Tibetan Buddhism (1935–)

85

DRINK IN MODERATION

Studies have shown that drinking one unit a day, especially of red wine, is linked to better physical health. In particular, the risks of heart disease during middle and old age are reduced. As well as the physical benefits, researchers have also found psychological benefits to moderate drinking, with moderate drinkers generally suffering lower rates of depression and anxiety than teetotallers. Here are some tips to keep your level of drinking healthy:

- Drink water and eat before you drink alcohol.
- Don't mix your drinks.
- Stick to the recommended limits.
- Never drink and drive.

86

GO ORGANIC

There are many advantages that make organic foods worth considering. Organic fruits and vegetables are free from pesticides, artificial fertilizers and food additives. Organic livestock must be reared without the routine use of antibiotics or growth hormones. Since some of the chemicals used in pesticides and growth hormones have been linked to cancer, some scientists believe organic food is better for health. Other studies suggest that organic foods contain higher levels of vitamins than their conventionally grown counterparts, since good-quality soil produces healthier plants.

87

DISCOVER MANUKA HONEY

Renowned for its healing properties, manuka honey is used to combat infections that have shown resistance to powerful antibiotics, such as the hospital superbug MRSA. It is produced in New Zealand from the manuka bush.

Manuka honey contains an extra, naturally occurring active component, which doesn't lose its potency when exposed to heat, light or dilution. The honey has antiviral and antibacterial actions, but it is not just used to soothe sore throats. Applied topically, it is an effective treatment for a variety of wounds and skin conditions, including acne, mouth ulcers, burns and insect bites. It can be bought from most health food stores.

88

HARVEST RAINWATER

Harvesting rainwater at home is an excellent way of conserving water, which is good for the environment and the cost savings make it good for you too. The simplest method is to buy a water butt, which is basically a bucket designed to catch precipitation, with a built-in hose to use when watering your garden. These can be bought online or in home and garden stores at a range of prices.

89

MAKE TRAVEL PLANS

Travel broadens our horizons, exposing us to unfamiliar cultures and offering new perspectives on life. By taking us away from our accustomed places and activities, it can lead to a reassessment of what's important. The prospect of travel may encourage us to learn a new language or to study the history of the places we hope to visit.

Adventurous travel does not have to involve long distances or huge expense. It can be just as rewarding to go on a local walking holiday as to fly to an exotic location on the other side of the world. Simply planning a trip or an expedition can be therapeutic. Poring over maps and guidebooks, surfing the net for ideas and making transport arrangements will heighten your sense of anticipation, and give you something to look forward to.

90

BRUSH UP YOUR SKIN

You can boost your circulation and improve the texture of your skin with some dry-skin brushing before you have a shower or bath each morning. Daily brushing using a loofah or long-handled natural-bristle brush will eliminate dead cells and unblock the pores, as well as kick-starting the lymph system. It is also a great way to combat cellulite.

Starting from the feet, brush the skin in long sweeps all the way up the body and along the limbs towards your heart to get the blood pumping. You will see the tiny dead cells floating away. Your skin will redden, but don't be alarmed. If you brush for just a few minutes every day, you will soon appreciate the benefits.

GROW CHILLI PEPPERS

Chillis boast a variety of health benefits, providing a great source of antioxidants and vitamins A and C. Grow your own chilli peppers to add some spice and a health kick to your soups, curries and sauces. Chillis can be sown in the late winter, but sowing seeds in spring will still yield a successful crop.

Fill small trays divided into little squares with potting soil, insert a seed and lightly cover with soil. Spray with water to avoid over-soaking and cover with a plastic lid. Keep in a warm, dark place. Once they have started to germinate, move them to another warm place, but this time with plenty of light; bring them away from windows at night or the drop in temperature may kill them.

When the seedlings grow to about 8–10 centimetres (3–4 inches), move them into individual pots and place them in a sunny, sheltered outside spot. Transplant them into bigger pots several times as they grow and water as required – the soil should never feel too wet.

Feed them with half-strength diluted liquid feed once or twice a week at first, then daily when the much-anticipated fruit starts to appear.

Confidence is Key
Learn to Jog
Relax and Unwind
Give Blood
Let Your Skin Breathe
Grow Tomatoes
Play More
Improve Your Posture
Natural Skin Moisturiser
Gargle with Oil
Try Rock Climbing
Take a Note for Yourself
Discover the Benefits of Garlic
Health Day
Enjoy the Sun
Loving Reminders
Wear Sunscreen
Have a Digital Detox
Savour Ginger
Eat Probiotic Yoghurt
Jettison Junk Mail
Limit Your Options
Stretch
Daily Inspiration
Be Open to Change
Use Olive Oil
Laugh More
Take the Stairs
Look After Your Kidneys
Eat Spices for Healthy Digestion
Try Foot Reflexology
Make Your Desk a Temple
Get in the Flow
Eat Mindfully
Travel by Public Transport
Monitor Your Skin
Natural Cooling Toner
Health Day
Curb Salt
Surround Yourself with Positive People
Have a Steam
Value Your Job
Daily Inspiration
Train the Brain
Improve Your Social Intelligence
Care for Your Hair Naturally
Health Day
Grow Herbs
Enjoy Your Time Alone
Shh…Keep it Quiet
Immerse Yourself in Music
Relax and Unwind
Daily Inspiration
Train the Brain
Make Breakfast Count
Resolve Family Disputes
Unplug it
Stretch
Take Your Pulse
Eat Raw Only Before Four
Have a Siesta
Stay Cool
Find a Thinking Space
Juice Day
Be Forgiving
Go Earthing
Love a Warm Climate
Pick Yourself Up
Enjoy the View
Natural Banana Mask
Observe Yourself
Keep a Food Journal
Grow Your Own Orchids
Soften Your Skin
Rediscover Kissing
Learn to Be Idle
Be Spontaneous
Eat Together
Strawberry and Cucumber Face Mask
Gorge on Grapefruit
Daily Inspiration
Health Day
Spend Less Time Grocery Shopping
Only Worry About Things You Can Change
Train the Brain
Savour Seaweed
Be Grateful
Host a Picnic
Stretch
Try Tea-Tree Oil
Become Emotionally Intelligent

SUMMER

Sunshine in moderation is good for all aspects of our wellbeing; warmer climates tend to make people happier, our bodies get a good dose of vitamin D and the sun's rays can even give our intelligence a boost. Therefore the summer months are ideal to find new ways to improve our lifestyles.

92

CONFIDENCE IS KEY

Confidence has a direct impact on mental and physical wellbeing. Some psychologists believe that confidence is a more powerful determinant of success than innate ability. It can make us more or less vulnerable to stress and depression, and it influences how far we are likely to persevere in the face of difficulties. It affects the immune system and activates endorphins, our natural painkillers.

Self-confidence is a set of beliefs about yourself, not an inherent skill or personality trait. You can be very competent and capable and still feel a lack of self-confidence, but it is possible to improve your confidence level, and it is worth trying to do so. Do this by focusing on the positives in your life. Recognise what you are good at and try to implement those things more into your daily routine.

93

LEARN TO JOG

Many people starting to jog take off too quickly. They race off down the road and then find they have to stop after 100 metres, gasping. The key to building a jogging regime is to begin slowly.

- Start barely faster than your walking workout pace and slowly gather speed from there.
- After 10 minutes or so, if you can keep the pace going, you will probably find that you start to settle into a rhythm and the whole jogging experience will feel more comfortable.
- Aim to do this for at least 20 minutes, three times a week. Gradually cut down on your walking time and jog more.

RELAX AND UNWIND: CUPPED-HAND CALMING

If you've been so busy burning the candle at both ends that it's been months since you had a few nights in with just the TV and a 9 o'clock curfew, what you need more than anything is some 'me time' to clear your mind. Simple mind-clearing exercises can help you relax, de-stress and banish any worries or fears that may have been lurking for some time.

- Find a quiet, comfortable place to sit. Place your cupped hands over your eyes, then close your eyes.
- Take a deep breath and concentrate on allowing the stresses and strains to leave your body.
- Hold this position for at least 10 breaths, then remove your hands from your eyes. Slowly open your eyes and focus on your surroundings.
- Remain seated comfortably for a few more minutes, enjoying the feeling of peacefulness.

95

GIVE BLOOD

Blood donors are always in demand. It can take 50 units of blood just to save one car accident victim and five units of blood for one cancer treatment. Beside the obvious altruistic reasons for donating blood, studies have shown that it may also have health benefits for the donor. By having blood removed from your body, you also remove excess iron. Iron oxidises cholesterol, which can lead to damaged arteries and heart disease. So roll up your sleeves for your heart, and somebody else's.

It's also beneficial to know your blood type as that will help you become aware of the health risks to which certain blood types may be predisposed. Also, if you're trying to conceive, knowing your own and your partner's blood type may help to avoid complications during pregnancy.

96

LET YOUR SKIN BREATHE

By ridding the skin of dead cells, exfoliating allows new skin cells to emerge, giving you a healthier glow and making your skin more responsive to treatments. Choose the correct exfoliant for you:

- Dry skin – a creamy exfoliant won't irritate the natural oils in dry skin or upset its sensitive balance.
- Normal skin – since normal skin is more resilient than other types, you can use an exfoliant with small granules in it.
- Oily skin – check that your exfoliant does not contain any irritants that may upset the pH balance or provoke skin eruptions.

97

GROW TOMATOES

Growing your own tomatoes is a delicious way to reduce your carbon footprint, and the growing process can be highly nurturing.

Fill a 7.5-centimetre (3-inch) pot with soil and lightly water. Scatter with a generous sprinkling of seeds and then add a thin layer of vermiculite – a natural mineral that insulates your seeds. Place on a sunny windowsill to germinate. You should see seedlings in two weeks, and the plants should be strong enough to move into their own pots at eight weeks.

To do this, hold each plant by its stem, gently digging into the soil to lift it out. Place each plant into its own 7.5-centimetre (3-inch) pot and water lightly. Once you can see roots coming through the drainage holes, transplant into a 12-centimetre (5-inch) pot. When the first branch of flowers appears, the tomato plants are ready to go into a larger pot, or growing bags.

98

PLAY MORE

Whether you are six or 106, play is beneficial, as well as being good fun. Scientists have suggested that play is essential to the successful development of both human and non-human species. It provides the young with chances to learn about the world and to experiment with new modes of behaviour.

It can be good for adults, too. Some experts suggest that play-fighting, for example, is a way of practising real-life hunting skills, which would have ensured human survival thousands of years ago.

IMPROVE YOUR POSTURE

Think about the shape of your spine at this very moment. Are you slumped over your desk? Uncomfortably perched on a chair? Is your pelvis crooked or twisted around your spine? If so, you could be putting your health at risk.

Now, sit upright. Plant your feet squarely on the floor and let your shoulders relax. Take some deep breaths. In these three short steps, you've taken positive action towards living a healthier life.

The body is a finely tuned piece of structural engineering. In order to work and move healthily, it needs to be properly aligned. A body out of line puts abnormal strain on muscles, tendons and ligaments, wearing out joints, bones and muscles, and perhaps affecting internal organs as well. Poor posture leads to lower back pain and osteoarthritis, among other back and spinal problems.

You can improve your posture by doing the following:

- Take up Pilates, try the Alexander technique or ask a gym trainer to devise a special programme for you. It's all about strengthening the muscles of your back and abdomen so that your spine can be held straight and upright.
- When you're at work, make sure that your desk or work area is ergonomically designed.
- Consciously break the slouching habit: if you notice yourself slouching, correct yourself and straighten your back.
- If you do suffer from back pain, seek advice from a physiotherapist, osteopath, chiropractor or back specialist – any of whom can recommend exercises to align your bones and muscles.

100

NATURAL SKIN MOISTURISER

If you have a tired complexion, use this cream twice a day after cleansing to help tighten pores and eliminate dead skin cells.

150g (1½ cups) almond oil
100g (1 cup) cocoa butter
1 teaspoon royal jelly
25g (¼ cup) beeswax
300ml (10 fl oz) distilled water
30 drops grapefruit extract oil

Combine the almond oil, cocoa butter, royal jelly and beeswax and melt over a low heat, stirring occasionally. Remove from the stove and add water. Blend until the mixture is thick and creamy. Add the grapefruit oil. Store in an airtight glass jar.

101

GARGLE WITH OIL

An oil mouthwash is an effective way of cleaning your palate that originates from Ayurvedic medicine. Use flaxseed oil or another kind of nut or seed oil for a few minutes to rinse away any toxins in the gums and to protect against gum disease. The method is, with your mouth, to pull or suck the oil through your teeth so that the oil loosens and picks up bacteria and particles between your teeth and gums. Do not swallow while you are doing this. Spit the oil out and rinse your mouth before brushing your teeth normally. Not all toxins will dissolve in water so rinse your mouth with oil regularly.

102

TRY ROCK CLIMBING

One exercise that will stretch your body and mind is rock climbing. It has increased in popularity over the years – both indoor and outdoor courses are available in even the most urban areas. It's a total body workout and burns almost 1,000 calories an hour, as well as toning your arms, shoulders, back, thighs and calves.

Women are usually very adept at picking up the tricks of rock climbing because their upper bodies are weaker than their male counterparts, and so they are used to using their legs as their main source of strength. You won't be allowed on a rock-climbing wall without first undergoing instruction, so book an introductory session before you begin. After the first time you reach the top of the wall, you'll be ready to come back for more.

103

TAKE A NOTE FOR YOURSELF

According to American psychologist Robert J. Sternberg, intelligence is about much more than vocabulary, memory and comprehension. It also includes creative and practical elements. Sternberg argues that analytical abilities allow us to evaluate, compare and contrast information. Creative abilities add invention and discovery to the mix. Practical abilities tie everything together by allowing individuals to apply what they have learned in the appropriate setting.

He suggests taking a pen and notebook wherever you go to jot down your ideas and look at them from different perspectives – practical or creative. Of course you can use a phone, tablet or laptop, too.

DISCOVER THE BENEFITS OF GARLIC

Garlic has been used all over the world as both food and medicine for thousands of years.

Scientific studies suggest that this humble bulb has many therapeutic benefits – it can help to reduce the risk of developing lung cancer, lower the risk of osteoarthritis and protect the heart from damage. Consuming garlic regularly can prevent infections of all kinds and even reduce the risk of catching the common cold.

It can also be used to detoxify the body, as it has sulphur-containing compounds that activate the liver enzymes responsible for expelling toxins.

Summer is garlic season and with its pungent, creamy flavour, it's a delicious way to pack more nutrients into your meals.

Try these simple recipes using raw and cooked garlic (raw is best):

- Purée fresh garlic with cannellini beans and tahini, olive oil and lemon juice to make a healthy dip.
- Add garlic and fresh lemon juice to steamed spinach, or other steamed vegetables.
- Roast whole garlic cloves, chop and add them to a creamy pasta salad.
- Combine parsley, citrus or mint with garlic to help sweeten the breath.

HEALTH DAY: SPINACH SALAD WITH GARLIC DRESSING

Spinach strengthens the blood and cleanses it of toxins – it's tasty raw or cooked. Add it to as many dishes as you can.

250g (2½ cups) baby spinach leaves
50g (½ cup) semi-dried tomatoes
4 slices sourdough baguette
Olive oil

Warm garlic dressing:

3 tablespoons olive oil
3 cloves garlic, sliced
2 tablespoons salted capers, rinsed
25g (¼ cup) olives
2 tablespoons lemon juice
2 tablespoons thyme leaves
Cracked black pepper

Place the spinach leaves and tomatoes on serving plates. Then put the baguette slices on a tray and drizzle with a little olive oil. Place under a hot grill and toast for one minute or until lightly browned.

To make the dressing, add the oil, garlic, capers, olives, lemon juice, thyme and pepper to a pan and cook for one minute or until heated through. Pour the warm dressing over the salad and top with the grilled baguette.

Serves four.

106

ENJOY THE SUN

Most people feel a great deal better when the sun shines. They are more cheerful, more optimistic, more able to deal with everyday problems – and they notice that other people are happier, too. Sunshine is also beneficial to health. The human body uses sunlight to create vitamin D, which protects against heart disease, rheumatoid arthritis and some types of cancer. Plus, it's long been recognised that sunshine (specifically bright light, rather than warmth) improves mood, by raising the level of serotonin produced by the brain.

Aim for a good balance: enough sun to enjoy its health benefits but not so much that it damages the skin. You will need to take into account season, latitude, time of day and your skin pigmentation. A rough guide to sensible exposure is 10 to 15 minutes of low-intensity sun on the arms, legs, hands or face, twice a week.

107

LOVING REMINDERS

Having mementos and reminders of your partner around you can help you feel close to them when you're apart. It can also relieve stress by triggering happy memories and experiences you've shared.

Choose a photo of the two of you together having fun and put it somewhere you can see it often. Use an image of your partner as your screensaver on your phone or computer, or carry a card or note from them that has special meaning to you. Having loving reminders around is a sure-fire way to brighten even the dullest day.

WEAR SUNSCREEN

Chances are that you love to relax in the warm summer sunshine. Who doesn't? It might also be the case that, on at least one occasion, you have been caught out. If so, you'll be familiar with the sensations associated with sunburn – tight, hot skin, inflamed and sore to the touch, followed by unsightly blistering. These are the things you can see or feel, but the health implications of burning in the sun are not always visible and can manifest over time.

Really, a suntan is a sign of the burning of the epidermis (the top layer of your skin). With continued exposure to the sun, your skin becomes thinner and more fragile and its connective tissues weaken, which in turn reduces your skin's strength and elasticity. Skin damage results in a condition called photoaging, which shows up in deep wrinkles, fine veins across the cheeks and nose, and patches of pigmentation such as tiny freckles and 'liver spots'. Here are other tips for protecting yourself from the sun:

- Cover up with suitable clothing.
- Wear a broad-brimmed hat or stay in the shade.
- Apply high-protection sunblock liberally and frequently.
- Always apply sunblock when swimming out of doors.
- Avoid the strongest sun in the middle of the day.
- Avoid such intense UV that you get sunburn.
- Do not use sunbeds and lamps.
- Get all strange spots and moles checked out early.

109

HAVE A DIGITAL DETOX

Technology makes up so much of our daily experience: we are constantly on our phones, checking our emails and social media pages and typing up reports. However, having a technology curfew in place every night can take the strain off your eyes and your mind. It can also limit the amount of electromagnetic waves that you absorb from your electronics.

Turn off your phone, tablet, laptop and any other distracting electronics at a set time in the evening and remove them from your bedroom. Instead, take time to reflect on your day, have a conversation with a loved one or read a book. A break from technology can feel refreshing and grounding, and it reminds you that there is a lot more to life than the contents of a small screen.

110

SAVOUR GINGER

Whether eaten fresh, sipped as a tea or taken as a nutritional supplement, ginger is a potent remedy for nausea, flatulence, vomiting and dizziness. Ginger is widely used for several other ailments:

- Ginger's anti-inflammatory and pain-relieving properties help to alleviate the muscle aches and chronic joint pain caused by rheumatoid arthritis.
- You can drink up to four cups of ginger tea a day to relieve the bronchial congestion associated with colds and flu.

111

EAT PROBIOTIC YOGHURT

'Probiotic' refers to the addition of live microorganisms that are beneficial for health. These are added to all yoghurts during the fermentation process, but yoghurts which are then heat-treated lose the active cultures and the benefits they provide. Some of these benefits include the restoration of a healthy gut wall and a boosted immune system.

Research has suggested that maintaining healthy intestinal flora makes it harder for 'bad' bacteria to populate the intestine, with the same believed true of the urinary tract. Probiotic intake is thought to improve digestive irregularities, and some strains are thought to reduce the symptoms of lactose intolerance. An extremely versatile superfood, probiotic yoghurt can be used as a substitute in recipes or combined with fruit and nuts for day-to-day use. Probiotics are also available in supplement form.

112

JETTISON JUNK MAIL

Junk mail is a global scourge that generates a stupendous waste of paper – and costs the planet 100 million trees each year. On average, in the Western world, people receive between 4 and 12 kilograms (8 and 26 pounds) of junk mail every year.

You can help stop this waste by following these tips:

- Don't join mailing lists.
- Always tick the no 'junk' box.
- Write back to the company and say 'no thank you'.

113

LIMIT YOUR OPTIONS

If you find decision-making a daunting task, you are not alone. In many cases, we are overwhelmed by our options and end up unhappy with our choices. Scientific studies at Columbia University have shown that, when faced with a large selection, people are more likely to feel dissatisfied or doubtful about their choice than when they make the same choice from a smaller range of alternatives.

Reducing the options you have to consider can save time and worry. Next time you're faced with an extensive menu of food, or need to buy an item and feel you must find the best, set a limit on your choices. Put a big mental cross through some options without deliberation. Sometimes finding the 'best' is unrealistic, so for a satisfied mind it's worth going for 'good enough'.

114

STRETCH: TRICEPS

Tricep exercises stretch the back of the arms, and help improve flexibility, circulation and the posture of the back, too.

- Stand tall with your feet hip-width apart and tummy tucked in.
- Bend your right elbow and reach your hand back so that it is resting on your right shoulder blade. Place your left hand on your right elbow and gently pull the elbow back. Keep your upper torso straight while you perform this stretch. Hold for 10 to 12 seconds, then repeat on the opposite arm.

DAILY INSPIRATION

'Continuous effort – not strength or intelligence – is the key to unlocking our potential.'

Winston Churchill
British politician (1874–1965)

116

BE OPEN TO CHANGE

Our lives today are driven by change – globalisation, new technology and the fast-moving nature of just about everything. People change too, our children grow up before our eyes and parents seem to age all too quickly.

Change in our lives is not just inevitable, it's an opportunity to grow and progress. Recognising this as a fact of life can be liberating and life-changing. Rather than being daunting, all of this newness can bring excitement and interest into our lives. At the same time, it can help us master fresh skills, gain knowledge and improve relationships.

Along with change come options, so recognise there will be unknowns and approach change positively with an open mind. The 'old' you will still be there, but in a new and improved form.

117

USE OLIVE OIL

People who have a typical Mediterranean diet suffer comparatively low rates of heart disease. Additionally, such a diet has been linked to a reduced death rate from all sorts of diseases and may also cut the risk of developing Alzheimer's disease.

One of the key ingredients of the Mediterranean diet is olive oil. It is a great idea to have two or three kinds in your kitchen. The highest quality is extra-virgin, which comes from the first pressing. But don't use it in cooking because heat will burn off its goodness; add it at the end.

LAUGH MORE

According to Madan Kataria, a doctor from Mumbai, India, children laugh on average 300 times a day but by adulthood this has dropped to an average of seven to 15 times a day. Researchers have shown that watching a comedic video can make the blood vessels expand, step up the blood flow by 22 per cent and leave viewers feeling wonderful. Since laughter benefits our physical and mental fitness in so many ways, it makes sense to laugh more often.

- Laughter reduces stress and depression.
- It relieves hay-fever symptoms, decreases pain, and allows us to tolerate discomfort more easily.
- It helps to protect against illness by increasing T-cells, which attack and kill tumour cells and viruses.
- It aids healing after operations and illnesses by stimulating the immune system.
- It reduces blood-sugar levels, which aids glucose tolerance for both diabetics and non-diabetics.
- It increases positive emotions, which in turn can boost creativity.
- It improves problem-solving skills.
- It releases tension and can even make unpleasant experiences more bearable.
- It may help to prevent heart attacks.

119

TAKE THE STAIRS

The next time you have the option of using a lift or escalator, instead consider taking the stairs. Even climbing a few flights of stairs a day can have a surprising impact on your health. Studies have shown that people who incorporated stair climbing into their workdays had a marked drop in weight and blood pressure after just a few months. Stairs are an easy (and cheap) way to incorporate exercise into your daily routine, especially if you do not have the time or money to go to a gym.

Though it is good to have a variety of aerobic exercises in your fitness regimen, stair climbing is one of the best that you can do. Stairs help build bone strength and tone muscles in the calves, thighs, buttocks and stomach. In fact, stair climbing is even more effective for toning and strengthening than running because running propels you mostly horizontally while stair climbing forces you to move vertically. The greater challenge placed on your muscles and bones to move against gravity makes them work harder. Stair climbing is also a low-impact activity, unlike running, which can strain your joints after several years.

Stair climbing is cheap, available to anyone who is situated near a staircase, not time-consuming and, above all, extremely effective in toning your muscles and raising your heart rate. Start slowly and build yourself up. Soon you may never see the inside of a lift again.

LOOK AFTER YOUR KIDNEYS

People with diabetes, high blood pressure and similar health problems are at risk of chronic renal disease, a condition that leads to the gradual destruction of the kidneys. Medical problems associated with the kidneys can also have a negative impact on mental faculties. One study identified a direct correlation between worsening kidney disease and slower brain responses; the researchers concluded that increasingly severe kidney disease is associated with progressive cognitive decline. The following are ways to keep your kidneys healthy:

- Eat plenty of fruit and vegetables as well as beans and grain-based food.
- Eat lean meat such as chicken and fish each week.
- Limit your intake of salty and fatty food.
- Drink plenty of water, which lessens the risk of kidney stones forming.
- Stay fit and maintain a healthy weight. Adults should exercise at a moderate pace for 30 minutes or more on most days.
- Don't smoke – it slows the flow of blood to the kidneys and increases the risk of kidney cancer.
- Limit your alcohol intake to two drinks per day if you are male and one drink per day if you are female.
- Have your blood pressure checked regularly, and discuss with your doctor any other appropriate medical tests, such as regular blood or urine tests.

EAT SPICES FOR HEALTHY DIGESTION

The process by which we digest food is very complex, requiring the coordination of many organs in order to effectively break down and absorb nutrients from food. A number of factors – such as stress, an unhealthy diet and alcohol – can affect your dietary system and prevent it from operating properly. If the digestive process loses its efficiency, it's possible for malnutrition or toxin build-up to occur. Some common symptoms of poor digestion are bloating, gas, constipation, diarrhoea and indigestion.

An effective way to alleviate these symptoms and promote healthy digestion is to incorporate a variety of herbs and spices into your diet. These flavourful ingredients range from familiar garden herbs – such as dill, bay, fennel, rosemary and oregano – to exotic spices – such as anise, coriander, ginger and cardamom.

The health benefits are numerous:

- Adding a dash of chilli peppers to your dinner will help boost your circulation.
- Sprinkling a few leaves of basil will give you an antioxidant lift.
- Adding a hint of cinnamon will also boost antioxidant levels.
- Herbs and spices can also be steeped in hot water to make a refreshing cup of tea.

By introducing such ingredients into your diet not only will you aid your digestion and increase your health and energy levels, but also you will make your food more flavourful without adding extra amounts of salt, fat and sugar.

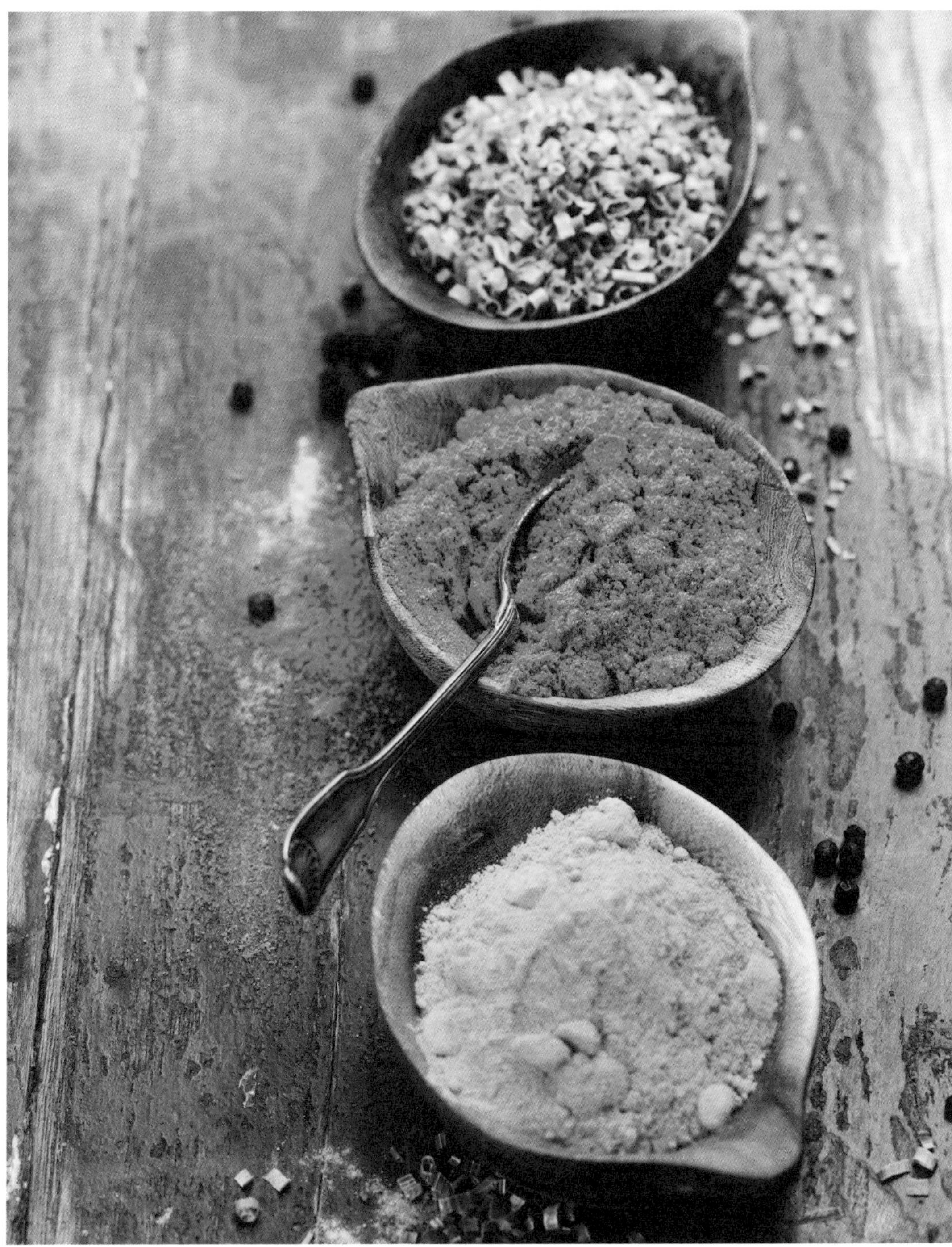

122

TRY FOOT REFLEXOLOGY

Treating your feet can have a relaxing, balancing, detoxing and healing effect on the whole body. This is because reflex areas in the feet correspond to internal organs. So give yourself a reflexology treatment. Here are some of the most important pressure points and the benefits that massaging them can bring:

Big toes: Helps to alleviate a headache

Ball of foot: Relieves tension in the neck and shoulders

Arch of foot: Relates to liver, bowel and kidney; this area may be tender if you've been burning the candle at both ends, so manipulate gently

Top of foot: Induces a state of psychological calm.

123

MAKE YOUR DESK A TEMPLE

According to a Princeton University study, a cluttered desk mentally exhausts you by restricting your ability to focus and limits your brain's ability to process information.

Treat your desk like a temple and clean it up. Arrange items so that you can see the desk surface. Go through your drawers and discard anything you don't use or need. Organise your shelves, keeping only a few personal items that have special meaning and motivate you. Keep your desk clean and germ-free and make it a food-free zone. Then sit back and enjoy your new workplace efficiency.

124

GET IN THE FLOW

Notice how musicians often seem to get lost in their music, eyes closed, as if in a trance-like state? This is known as 'flow' – when people are so fully absorbed in what they are doing that they don't notice what's going on around them and afterwards they feel great. Athletes describe it as being 'in the zone'.

Finding your flow is a pathway to achieving greater satisfaction and happiness by releasing you from self-consciousness. Music is not the only way to get in tune. In fact, any activity you enjoy can work, though it must be something that challenges without taxing you, and which you can really concentrate on.

Different things work for different people, so aim to find an activity that absorbs you and set aside 30 minutes every few days to let yourself get carried away.

125

EAT MINDFULLY

More often than not we eat mind*less*ly – shovelling down food at lunch while we type at our computers, mechanically chewing and swallowing as we watch a television programme at dinner. But eating mindfully – which means paying attention to the tastes, smells, textures and sensations of the food you eat without distraction – has surprising benefits. Taking time to concentrate on your food not only makes the experience of eating more enjoyable, but it can also improve your digestion and even train your body to feel satisfied on less. So at your next meal, sit down and really focus on what you're eating. You may find you feel better and fuller.

TRAVEL BY PUBLIC TRANSPORT

Switch from driving to public transport for just one day and you'll make an immediate difference. A single person can save about 9 kilograms (20 pounds) of carbon dioxide per day, according to a study carried out by the American Public Transport Association. That adds up to about 2 metric tons (about 2 ¼ short tons) per year.

A full underground train can remove more than 2,000 vehicles from the road. Because of its efficiency, many governments are actively pursuing public transport as the only way to lower pollution, traffic and greenhouse gases.

Here are some of the benefits of public transport:

- Public transport lowers pollution.
- Using it produces 95 per cent less carbon monoxide, about 50 per cent less carbon dioxide and 50 per cent fewer nitrogen oxides per mile compared to cars.
- Public transport increases property values. Homes that are located near public transport and so linked to local amenities are often worth considerably more (studies show house prices increase by 13 to 45 per cent depending on the city and neighbourhood).
- Public transport is also safer, according to the United States National Safety Council. Each mile travelled by car yields 25 times more fatal accidents compared to the same distance travelled on public transport. Injury rates are also lower per mile.

127

MONITOR YOUR SKIN

The most important aspect of monitoring skin health is to look out for signs of skin cancers (melanomas). These can be very aggressive, can spread quickly and are hard to treat unless caught early. Malignant melanoma has been increasing faster than any other type of tumour. To decrease your risk of developing skin cancer, protect yourself from the harmful effects of UV exposure.

Examine yourself once a month – ideally in a well-lit room in front of a full-length mirror. Check your face, ears, neck, chest and belly. Women should lift each breast in turn to check the skin underneath. Check both sides of your arms, the tops and palms of your hands and your fingernails. Inspect the bottoms of feet, calves and the backs of thighs. Use a hand-held mirror to inspect your neck, shoulders, upper arms, back and lower body.

128

NATURAL COOLING TONER

Cucumber reduces puffiness, while chamomile soothes your skin.

1 cucumber
½ carrot
60ml (¼ cup) chamomile tea
120ml (½ cup) lemon juice

Juice the cucumber and carrot. Add chamomile tea and lemon juice. Combine all the ingredients in a jar and shake. Use a cotton-wool ball to apply to your face. Keep refrigerated and use within three days.

HEALTH DAY: ZINGY AVOCADO SALAD

The humble avocado pear packs a great punch when it comes to your health. Firstly, it is high in fibre – both soluble and insoluble. The soluble fibre makes you feel fuller for longer after eating, while the insoluble fibre is a great aid to digestion. Secondly, avocados are also high in protein and vitamin E and provide one-third of the daily recommendation for vitamin C. Finally, they also contain glutathione, an antioxidant that fights free radicals.

If you are watching your weight, you might be tempted to avoid eating avocados because they are fattening, but you'd be making a mistake. While it is true that they are high in fat (on average half an avocado contains 15 grams (0.5 ounces) of monounsaturated fat and 2 grams (0.06 ounces) of saturated fat), the pros far outweigh the cons. Considered heart-healthy since it helps to lower cholesterol, monounsaturated fat can also help to reduce inflamed skin conditions, such as eczema, acne or psoriasis.

- 1 navel orange, peeled
- 1 ripe avocado, stoned and peeled
- 2 ripe tomatoes
- ½ spring onion
- 2 tablespoons salad dressing
- 3 to 4 black olives

It is best to peel the orange using a sharp knife – you want to remove all of the pith. Dice the orange, avocado and tomato into equal sized chunks – not too small. Thinly slice the spring onion. Place all of the ingredients in a bowl and stir to combine. Serve at room temperature.

Serves one.

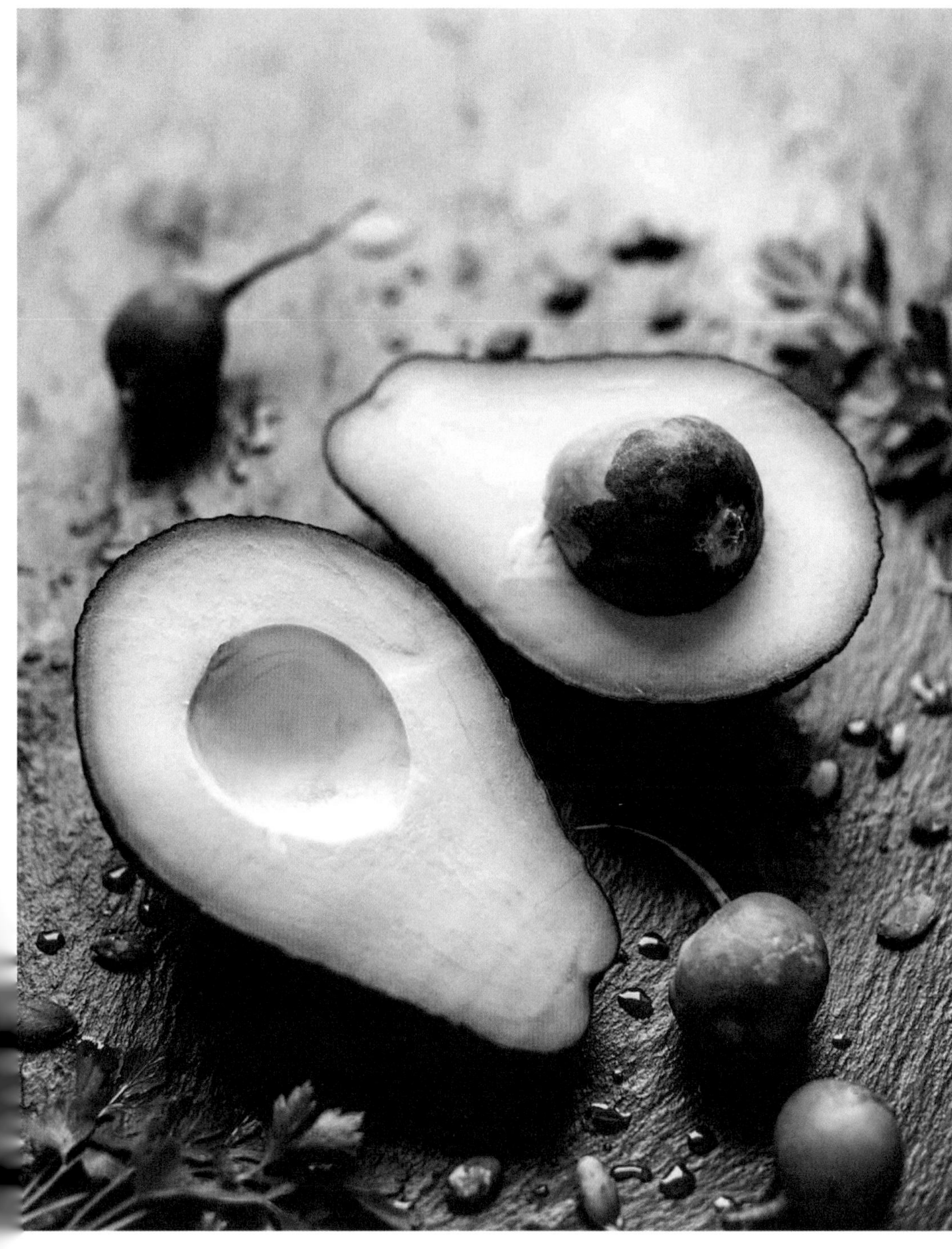

130

CURB SALT

High salt intake is particularly dangerous because it increases the risk of heart disease and strokes. Adults should consume no more than 6 grams (0.25 ounce) of salt per day, but in reality many of us exceed this figure regularly. This is largely due to the hidden salts in our modern diets. The less salt we eat, the less salt we will crave, and the first step to reducing salt intake is being aware.

- When cooking, try using alternative seasonings, such as black pepper or fresh herbs and spices, which will transform the flavour and add variety to your dish.
- Incorporate foods that naturally contain lower salt levels, such as chicken, mozzarella cheese, fruits, vegetables and plain rice.
- Check nutrition labels for reduced-salt options when choosing ready meals, bread, pasta sauces and soups.

131

SURROUND YOURSELF WITH POSITIVE PEOPLE

Positive people are those who make you feel happy, special, empowered or confident. Exposing yourself to and engaging with positive people will make you feel happier and may help eradicate the more 'toxic' relationships in your life.

Developing strong relationships and building support communities have been shown vastly to improve the quality and length of a person's life. By really paying attention to your relationships and actively surrounding yourself with positive people, you will be taking steps to a happier existence.

132

HAVE A STEAM

A steam room is basically a 'wet air room', in which wet air infiltrates the lungs and slows the production of bacteria or viruses. The steam opens up the airways in the lungs, making breathing much easier. Steam rooms that use aromatherapy oils such as tea tree or eucalyptus can also help to accelerate the relaxation process and eliminate bacteria.

If you suffer from scaly skin or pustules, steam rooms can help loosen dead skin. Spend a few minutes in the steam room, followed by a warm shower. Gently rub the affected area with a loofah. This should loosen the flaky skin, leaving you with smooth, baby-soft skin. Don't rub too hard though, as your skin will be especially sensitive after the heated room. Stay in for no longer than 20 minutes, although shorter bursts are preferable.

133

VALUE YOUR JOB

Employed people tend to be happier than unemployed people. Even if you don't think of your job as a vocation, you may value the fact that it gives you independence and status in your community, allows you to take care of your family or enables you to pursue your favourite leisure activity.

For many people, a job is also an important source of social relationships and self-esteem, so losing a job can be devastating. Not only does your income go down, but you lose all the intangible benefits as well. Scientists who have studied this subject suggest that the monetary costs of sudden unemployment are very small compared with the non-monetary costs.

DAILY INSPIRATION

'When one door of happiness closes, another opens, but often we look so long at the closed door that we do not see the one that has been opened for us.'

Helen Keller
American author, political activist, lecturer (1880–1968)

135

TRAIN THE BRAIN: NUMBER TEASERS

Keep your mind sharp with number puzzles; see how quickly you can solve the ones below.

1: A car leaves Toronto at 6.20 p.m. and arrives in Detroit, 180 miles away, at 10.05 p.m. What is its average speed in miles per hour?

2: Mary is 32 years old. She is four times as old as her brother. How old will Mary be when she is twice as old as her brother?

Answers: 1. 48 mph. There are 225 minutes between 6.20 p.m. and 10.05 p.m. If you divide 180 miles by 225 minutes, you find the average speed of the car in miles per minute (0.8). If you multiply this by 60 you get the average speed in miles per hour.
2. 48 years old. Mary's brother is currently eight years old (because 4 x 8 = 32). In 16 years time, Mary will be 48 and her brother will be 24.

136

IMPROVE YOUR SOCIAL INTELLIGENCE

According to the psychologist Howard Gardner, there are nine types of intelligence. One of the most significant types is social intelligence – the ability to understand and interact with others.

Other psychologists argue that, in modern society, outstanding leaders need a combination of self-mastery and social intelligence.

It appears that social intelligence becomes increasingly significant as human societies become more complex. And some scientists argue that the ability to learn from others may have played a pivotal role in the evolution of the human brain.

CARE FOR YOUR HAIR NATURALLY

As one of the most sensitive parts of the human body, the scalp requires a high level of care and consideration. Surprisingly, many hair products – like hair dyes, hairsprays, shampoos and conditioners – often contain a damaging cocktail of chemicals. In addition to artificial colours and fragrances, common ingredients in hair products include ammonia and formaldehyde. Continual exposure to these chemicals can have a wide range of unwanted effects, from minor skin irritation to more harmful ailments such as cancer.

You can avoid exposing yourself to these harmful chemicals by using natural, organic hair products, which are increasingly available in health food stores. However, you can just as easily make your own hair products at home using common kitchen items. Bicarbonate of soda makes an effective and affordable shampoo – simply rub a mixture of water and bicarbonate of soda from your scalp to the tips of your hair and let it sit for a few minutes before rinsing. Not only does it outperform many commercial shampoo products, but also it doesn't leave chemical residue in your hair after washing. If you're looking for a new hair colour, look no further than your fridge or pantry: hair can be lightened by applying lemon juice or darkened using tea.

HEALTH DAY: LENTIL, BROCCOLI AND MANGETOUT SALAD

Easy to incorporate into any dish and with many health benefits, broccoli contains at least 50 per cent more vitamin C than oranges and is also an excellent source of fibre. Studies have linked broccoli and other non-starchy vegetables to lower incidences of cancer and heart disease.

200g (1 cup) Puy lentils
1 litre (1¾ pint) vegetable stock
140g (¾ cup) broccoli
140g (4.9 oz) mangetout
140g (4.9 oz) edamame beans

For the dressing:

1 clove garlic
2 tablespoons rapeseed oil
Juice 1 lemon
2 tablespoons soy sauce
½ teaspoon red chilli flakes
1 tablespoon honey

Cook the lentils in the stock for 15 minutes, until tender but not disintegrating. Drain and set aside to cool. Cut the broccoli into small florets. Bring a large saucepan of water to the boil and blanch the broccoli, mangetout and edamame beans for two minutes. Drain and refresh under cold water.

To make the dressing, peel and crush the garlic, and combine with all the remaining ingredients. Mix well. Toss the cooked vegetables, lentils and dressing together and serve chilled.

Serves four.

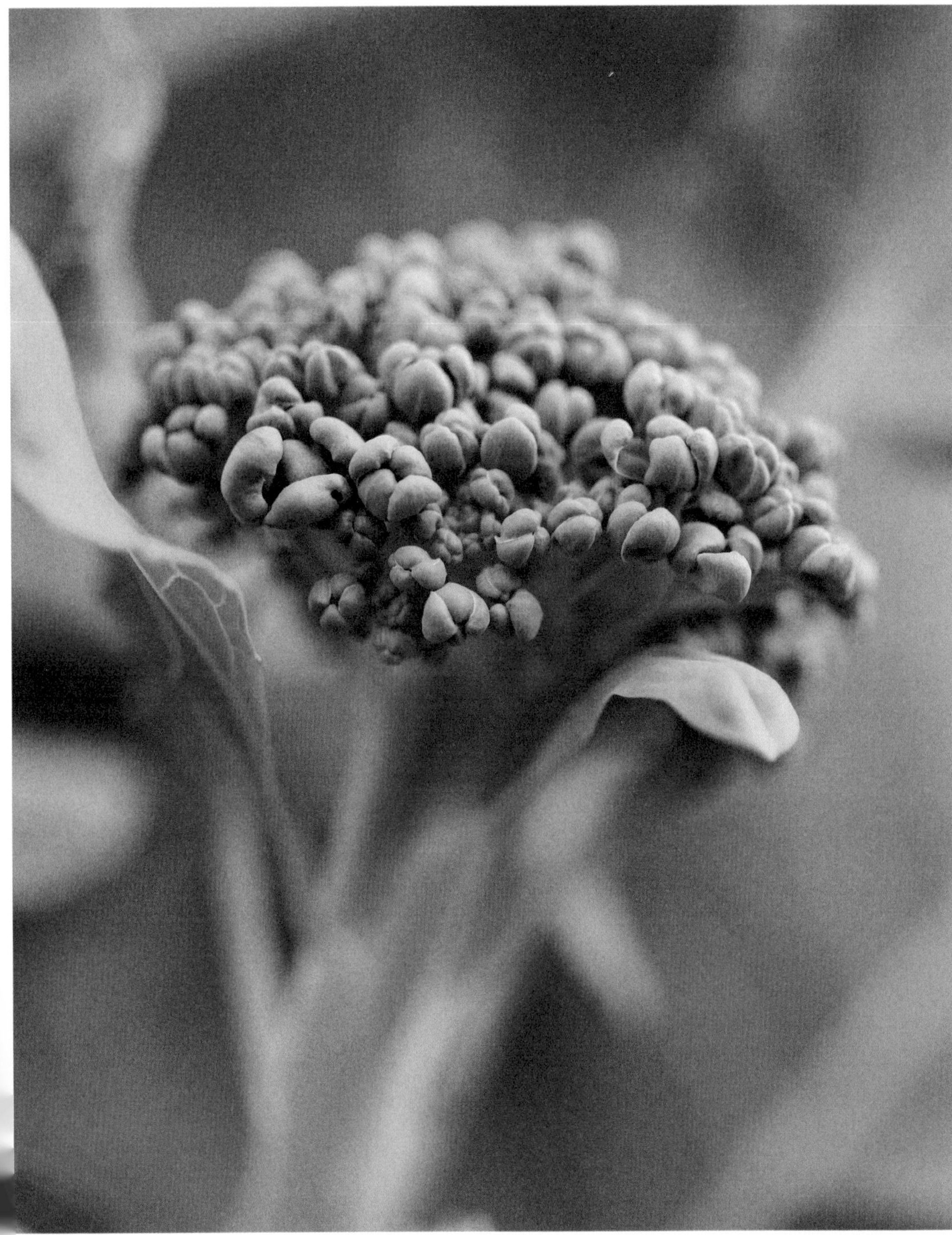

139

GROW HERBS

It is a known fact that many herbs have medicinal properties. Some aid the digestive system (oregano and mint), others give immunity a boost (rosemary and thyme) and a number are natural antiseptics (sage and bay). Even without their medicinal properties however, herbs add a fragrant touch to a meal and offer a healthy alternative to salt for seasoning. By growing your own herbs you will increase the choices you have when it comes to cooking and will always have a wonderful fragrance within arm's reach.

Buy ready-grown herbs from a supermarket or garden centre and repot them for your patio or windowsill. They will grow in almost any container, as long as there is plenty of drainage (placing some small stones at the bottom of the container will help with this). Pack your plants in tightly – they will look better and, as long as you prune and water them regularly and bring them indoors for winter, they will grow well. The amount of water they need varies depending on the type of herb and where it is being kept, so check the containers regularly and water them if the soil feels dry to the touch.

140

ENJOY YOUR TIME ALONE

Without a few quiet moments alone to reflect on your life, you may find yourself feeling stressed, unmotivated and resentful, and these emotions can have negative effects on your psychological and physical health.

Time alone allows you to recharge and breathe, and planning and setting personal goals alone lets you think clearly and independently about what will make you happy, away from the influence of others.

If you are not used to having alone time, you may have to make a conscious effort to build it in to your schedule. Allot yourself at least half an hour of alone time a day; try waking up half an hour early so that you can enjoy a quiet morning to yourself.

141

SHH ... KEEP IT QUIET

Noise is responsible for a type of chronic stress that puts the body into a state of raised alert. Even when you are asleep, your body continues to react to sounds, pumping out stress hormones such as cortisol and epinephrine. These hormones can cause changes to the heart and blood vessels which contribute to high blood pressure, heart failure, heart attacks and stroke. The threshold for cardiovascular problems is a chronic noise exposure of 50 decibels or above (a little less than might be expected in a busy restaurant). Constant low-level background noise can also raise stress levels – a mere 35 decibels of background noise is enough to raise the risks.

IMMERSE YOURSELF IN MUSIC

In 1993, the idea that listening to Mozart could boost your intelligence gained a great deal of attention after researchers found that 36 university undergraduates improved their ability to mentally manipulate objects in three-dimensional space after listening to 10 minutes of a sonata written by the great composer. Suddenly, the 'Mozart Effect' was born, spawning a veritable industry of recordings that promised to boost intelligence. In the years since that first report the conclusions of the original research have often been overstated. Researchers who tried to repeat the initial study failed to get the same results. Others have reviewed a wide range of different studies and found that overall the impact of listening to Mozart was not significant.

And yet, there are many researchers who still believe that listening to music can enhance your overall cognitive arousal and your ability to concentrate. One Belgian group, for example, found that a music-based exercise programme could improve cognitive function in a group of women with dementia.

In 2006, researchers reported in the Annals of the New York Academy of Sciences that listening to any music you find enjoyable has positive effects on cognition. The study actually found that the spatial abilities of 10- and 11-year-olds improved when the children were allowed to listen to pop music, but not when they were played Mozart. So if you happen to enjoy Mozart, by all means play his music. If you don't, perhaps sticking to what you like might be more effective.

RELAX AND UNWIND: RELAXATION POSITION

In all floor exercises it is vital to prepare your mind and body for exercise and be aware of body alignment.

- Lie flat on your back. Bend your knees and place your feet on the floor hip-width apart. Place your hands on your abdomen. Feel your body relaxing into the floor, your muscles softening and your spine lengthening. Relax your jaw and facial muscles.
- Roll your pelvis slowly from one side to another. Then roll your pelvis slowly back and forth until you find your 'neutral pelvis'.
- The pelvis is the base of support for your body. Its position can affect your spinal alignment and posture. Viewed from the side, the pelvis should be held in a way that maintains the normal concave curve of the lower back of the spine: the lumbar curve. If the pelvis tips forward or back, it can create back strain.
- Finding your neutral pelvis means defining the place where your spine rests while preserving all its natural curves. While reasonably easy to do when standing up, such alignment is more difficult when lying down.

DAILY INSPIRATION

'Take care of your body. It's the only place you have to live.'

Jim Rohn
American author and motivational speaker (1930–2009)

145

TRAIN THE BRAIN: PUZZLE CHALLENGE

Regularly doing crosswords and solving other puzzles can help to keep your cognitive powers in good shape as you grow older. How long do these puzzles take you to complete?

1: There are a total of 31 matches in a knock-out tennis tournament. Once a player loses a match, he or she is out of the tournament. How many players take part in the tournament?

2: Your bedroom clock is broken. Every hour it gains 36 minutes. However, exactly one hour ago it stopped, showing the time as 8.24 a.m. You know that it showed the correct time at 2 a.m. What time is it now?

Answers: 1. 32 players take part in the tournament. 2. It is 7 a.m.

146

MAKE BREAKFAST COUNT

Some people shun breakfast because they think it will help them lose weight. In fact, research shows that eating breakfast can help you to control your weight. A healthy breakfast is an important part of a balanced diet and provides some of the vitamins and minerals we need for good health.

Porridge made with semi-skimmed milk is an excellent choice – the oats are a good source of insoluble fibre and release energy slowly, making you feel fuller for longer. Another great option is muesli, fresh fruit and low-fat yoghurt, which provides calcium, protein and antioxidants.

147

RESOLVE FAMILY DISPUTES

If you have brothers and sisters, you probably quarrelled when you were children. Perhaps you borrowed each other's toys or clothes without asking, or got each other into trouble with your parents. These hostilities can resurface again in later life, particularly at times of family tension.

Conflict between teenagers and their parents is almost inevitable, but family differences have been shown to have an adverse effect on teenagers' wellbeing. Conversely, resolving conflicts with parents is linked to greater wellbeing when measured in terms of self-esteem, incidence of depression and the likelihood of risky behaviour such as drinking.

So if you have family conflicts, it is worth taking the time to resolve them, and making the effort to spend time as a family.

148

UNPLUG IT

A great deal of energy is wasted by leaving electronic household appliances in standby mode. In fact, the power used to keep display clocks lit and memory chips active accounts for between five and eight per cent of total domestic energy consumption.

You could buy low-standby devices or, even better, turn off the devices altogether. If you have several appliances in one room, use a multi-socket extension lead with an on/off switch. Always remember when leaving a room to switch off the lights, turn off the television or stereo and unplug any charging devices that are not being used.

STRETCH: DOWNWARD-FACING DOG

Downward-facing dog is good for warming up the body and giving your heart a rest. The pose stretches and releases tension in the upper spine and neck, and strengthens and stretches the upper body. It also stimulates the brain and nervous system.

- Start off on your hands and knees on the floor. Curl your toes under and straighten your legs slowly, pushing your buttocks up into the air and inhaling as you do so.
- Press backwards on your hands, so that you are pressing your chest toward the floor. Hold for a few breaths and then lower gently back to your knees. Repeat three or four times.
- If you're just beginning to practise yoga or you aren't flexible enough yet, don't force your heel to the floor or you will overstretch your Achilles tendon. If your back is at all sore, keep your knees bent. Take extra care if you have arthritic wrists.

150

TAKE YOUR PULSE

Checking your pulse can give you an indication of your fitness level and the state of your general health.

Find the soft area on the inside of your wrist below the base of your thumb and next to the tendons that run up your forearm. Press two fingers (not a thumb) lightly on this area. You will feel the pulse of blood pushing through the veins. Count the number of pulses for one minute. Your resting pulse rate simply gives you an indication of what your heart is doing at times when you are not exercising. For perfect accuracy, you should take your pulse when you first wake up in the morning. These are average pulse measurements:

- A fit pulse is in the range of 50 to 60.
- An average to fair fitness level will display a pulse rate of 61 to 75.
- Poor fitness will display a pulse rate of 75+.

151

EAT RAW ONLY BEFORE FOUR

Raw or uncooked vegetables and fruits are packed with enormous health benefits – they often contain heat-sensitive nutrients that burn off during cooking. However, raw foods are naturally more difficult for your body to digest because of the insoluble fibre they contain. By eating raw foods earlier on in the day, you have a better chance of digesting them fully, preventing issues such as bloating, gas and stomach pain that can result when food is left to ferment in your digestive tract. To give your system a rest, eat raw foods before four o'clock in the afternoon, and after this only eat foods that are completely cooked.

152

STAY COOL

You can feel the sun on your skin and the grass beneath your feet. Your spirit soars, your muscles relax, you just feel better. While you're having fun, avoid dehydration, sun damage and heat-related illnesses from fluid and electrolyte (salts) loss through heavy sweating. Here are some easy ways to stay cool on a summer day:

- Hydrate regularly with cool water, fruit juices and chilled herbal teas (limit your intake of alcohol).
- Slip on a shirt, slop on the sunscreen and slap on a hat.
- Rest under a shady tree and lose yourself in a book.
- Use aloe vera gel to soothe sunburn and moisturise sun-kissed skin.
- Find a beach, pool or river and go for a cooling swim.

153

FIND A THINKING SPACE

Creating a personal thinking space is a useful way to stimulate your creativity and help you sort through life's stresses. This space can be anywhere from a shady corner of your back garden to a quiet café. Make it a ritual to go to this place and centre yourself as you focus on what's important in your life. Get your creative juices flowing, or devote a few minutes to deciding on a course of action. Practise this habit for a while and you will come to associate it with a greater sense of control over your thoughts and more constructive outcomes.

HAVE A SIESTA

Staying at the top of your game during a long working day is a big challenge. The good news is that having a brief sleep, even one that lasts just a few minutes, can make a world of difference to your mental state.

A number of studies have been conducted: one research team studied the impact of a 10-minute nap on the alertness and cognitive function of 16 healthy volunteers. They found that it left the participants more alert and better able to perform intellectual tests. In another study, seven young adults found that a 20-minute sleep in the afternoon improved their performance level and their confidence in carrying out tasks. Yet another group of researchers showed that napping for 15 minutes improved logical reasoning.

Indeed, humans may be naturally predisposed to sleeping in small snatches during the day. Solo sailors, who have to strive against the elements around the clock, tend to sleep for short intervals ranging from 20 minutes to two hours.

All this makes sense when you consider the popularity of the siesta – the midday rest that has long been part of the culture in many regions of the world, especially where it is hot and sunny in the middle of the day.

The trick to successful napping seems to be to get enough sleep to revive yourself without sinking into such a deep sleep that you are left feeling groggy afterwards.

JUICE DAY: STRAWBERRY STAR

Strawberries, which are high in antioxidants, can help banish the 'stains' on your health caused by excessive alcohol consumption and nicotine.

- 5 strawberries, hulls removed
- Handful of blueberries
- Handful of raspberries
- 1 banana
- 1 tablespoon plain probiotic yoghurt
- Handful of pumpkin and sunflower seeds
- 425ml (1¾ cups) apple juice (freshly juiced or 100 per cent pure fruit juice)

Combine all ingredients in a blender. Blend until seeds are completely mixed in. Pour into a tall glass, and add ice if desired.

Serves one.

156

BE FORGIVING

Studies show that the act of forgiving reduces anger, hostility, depression, anxiety and negative emotions. In addition, forgiving people are more likely to be happier, more agreeable and more serene. Forgiveness is also linked to physical health benefits such as a reduction in blood-pressure levels.

- Imagine forgiving a wrongdoer – and see how much better you feel as a result.
- Write a letter of forgiveness (you don't have to send it).
- Practise empathising with other people in your daily life. If someone behaves in a way you don't understand, don't jump to conclusions.

157

GO EARTHING

Also known as 'Earthing' or 'Grounding', walking barefoot has recently been shown to offer both physiological and psychological benefits. A study published in 2012 in the *Journal of Environment and Public Health* discusses the antioxidant effects of direct contact between feet and electrons on the earth's surface. It found that stimulating nerve endings on the bottom of feet in this process helps drain free radicals from the body. The study also confirmed that Earthing decreases blood pressure, reduces inflammation and can even improve irregular sleep. Just a short barefoot walk around your garden will reconnect you with nature, heighten your awareness of your surroundings and stimulate your sense of touch.

LOVE A WARM CLIMATE

The climate in which we live exerts a crucial influence on our health. Extreme cold weather brings the threat of exposure, hypothermia and infections such as influenza, bronchitis and pneumonia, while excessively hot weather can put intolerable strain on the heart and cause problems with dehydration. Very old and very young people are most vulnerable, especially from diseases such as seasonal flu.

Somewhere between the extremes is the ideal climate, where the winters are mild and the summers are pleasantly warm. Research into 'Blue Zones' – areas of the world where people live measurably longer – has identified the Mediterranean island of Sardinia as one of these places. A remarkably high proportion of people who live there reach their one-hundredth year, including, unusually, a large number of men – there are 13.56 centenarians per 100,000 people in this balmy region. An attractive alternative is Okinawa in Japan, where the temperature hovers around and above 20° Celsius (68° Fahrenheit) for most of the year and, amazingly, more than 40 out of 100,000 people are over 100 years old.

The critical aspect of these statistics seems to be that many of those who reach the age of 80 proceed to survive for much longer – they are entering a period of life in which human beings are most sensitive to the effects of climate and least able to cope with harsh conditions.

159

PICK YOURSELF UP

In general, people with a high level of self-esteem put considerable effort into looking after their health and wellbeing. There are several positive steps you can take to build up your self-esteem if it is at a low ebb:

- Start by making a list of your good points, and don't be hard on yourself. Once you have your list, abandon modesty and congratulate yourself on these points every day.
- Doing something kind for others has been shown to increase self-esteem, so find a community group you can volunteer with, preferably one that interests you.
- Spend time with people who reinforce your belief in yourself, and avoid those who threaten your self-esteem by being negative or thinking themselves superior.

160

ENJOY THE VIEW

Research has shown that after an operation, those patients who were assigned to hospital rooms with an appealing outdoor view recovered faster and were discharged sooner than those who had no view.

A beautiful view helps all of us to keep healthy by lifting our mood, easing stress and providing a deep sense of optimism and contentment. So place your chair by the window and have a good look outside.

161

NATURAL BANANA MASK

Bananas are a rich source of magnesium, potassium, iron, zinc, iodine and vitamins A, B, E and F. This mask is an ideal rejuvenating treatment for skin of all ages.

- 1 small banana
- 2 tablespoons thick cream
- 1 tablespoon honey
- 1 tablespoon wholemeal flour
- Bottled or spring water

Mash the banana and add cream, honey and flour. Mix well. You may need to add more cream or flour to obtain the right consistency. Apply the mask to a clean face, making sure that you include the area around the eyes and the neck, and leave on for 30 minutes. Rinse off with water and pat your face dry.

162

OBSERVE YOURSELF

It's hard to be completely objective when considering our own lives and difficulties. Often, we fall into the trap of overthinking things, or seeing the situation through the filter of our own emotions, prejudices and assumptions. A deceptively simple way to achieve a major shift in your thinking – often to a more positive and realistic position – is to imagine you are someone from outside your circle of acquaintances looking at your situation. Try to see what they would see, with no judgements or preconceptions, and you'll potentially gain a whole new perspective on yourself. The results can be transformative.

KEEP A FOOD JOURNAL

Food journalising, particularly if you're on a diet, is a useful way to see what and how much you really eat. But beyond that, food journalising can give you accurate insight into how you eat emotionally and how the food you eat affects your body.

- By recording and quantifying every item of food that passes between your lips, you make yourself more accountable for your diet.
- You may be motivated to make better decisions because you can actually see where your calories are coming from and how nutritional your choices are.
- Note how you are feeling before, during and after your meal, so you can pinpoint your emotional triggers and actively work to counter any negative habits.
- A food journal is also a useful tool for tracking food allergies. Scribble down any reactions you have to your food, and patterns may arise that you can talk about with your doctor.

But you must be honest with your food journal. Don't think you can simply ignore that chocolate biscuit that you snuck in before lunch. Remember, the journal's effectiveness runs on your discipline and honesty. Use a journal platform that works for you and your busy life, whether that is a notebook that you can carry around in your handbag or an online database on your computer or smartphone. At first you may find it difficult to maintain a food journal, but once you get used to recording your meals, you will find that they lead you to a greater understanding of your food and your body.

GROW YOUR OWN ORCHIDS

Photosynthesis in plants involves taking in carbon dioxide and releasing oxygen, a process that is reversed at night-time in most plants. One exception to this rule is the orchid, which continues to take in carbon dioxide and release oxygen at night, making orchids a particularly good choice for a bedroom.

Some orchids are beautiful to look at but notoriously tough to grow. Ask for advice at your local garden centre on the variety best suited to the environment you can provide.

- Ensure good air circulation and effective drainage for orchid roots, but do not repot a flowering orchid.
- Give the plant plenty of light but avoid exposure to direct midday sunlight – they do not like dry heat.
- Mist with a fine spray once or twice a week.
- Water generously every seven to 10 days with tepid water. Keep the soil moist but not wet. Never allow an orchid to become waterlogged.
- Occasionally apply heavily diluted fertilizer but only when the plant is in active growth.
- When the plant has finished flowering, cut stems diagonally just above the third or fourth leaf node. A new stem can sometimes take up to six months to appear, so be patient.

165

SOFTEN YOUR SKIN

You'll be amazed at how soft and smooth your skin feels after a sugar treatment. Regular use of this scrub, along with a loofah, is particularly recommended if you suffer from small red bumps.

- 250g (1¼ cups) white cane sugar
- 250ml (8.8 fl oz) avocado oil
- 2 teaspoons aloe vera gel
- 2 drops lavender essential oil
- 2 drops orange essential oil

Combine the ingredients in a bowl. Scoop out some of the mixture and massage gently into your skin for one minute. Leave on for three to four minutes before rinsing. Any blotchiness that develops after using the scrub will be temporary.

166

REDISCOVER KISSING

In the early days of a loving relationship, kissing is often intense and provocative, but it may be neglected over time. It can be an important part of connecting as a couple, and the lack of this act of intimacy can have a negative effect on your relationship and your happiness. So if you think you've been sparing with your affection, it might be time to rediscover kissing.

LEARN TO BE IDLE

Apart from being pleasurable, doing nothing in a mindful way is an excellent way to enhance wellbeing. When we replace scattered thoughts with focused attention, the calming and restorative effects can be transformative.

Mindfulness and particularly meditation have been scientifically proven to reduce stress, improve memory and enhance creativity and overall feelings of wellbeing. The more you practise, the easier it becomes to enjoy the benefits of a calm, focused mind.

An easy way to begin is to sit in nature and contemplate a beautiful scene. The simple act of looking at a single bloom in your garden for a minute or two can produce a profound feeling of calm and relaxation. Stroking a pet and focusing on the sensation of touch can achieve the same effect. The important thing is to use single-minded attention and focus on one thing only.

So put away the to-do lists, shut down technology, find a quiet spot and just be.

Here's a simple 10-minute exercise you can use to practise resting the mind:

Sit or lie in a comfortable position in a quiet place where you won't be disturbed for 10 minutes or so.

Quieten your thoughts and take a few deep breaths in and out, concentrating on the sound of your breathing and the flow of air through your nostrils.

If unwanted thoughts come up, observe them briefly, then go back to the breathing and let them pass.

Remain like this for around 10 minutes, or longer if possible.

Gently refocus on your surroundings and enjoy the sense of calm you have achieved.

168

BE SPONTANEOUS

Finding time to pursue your hobbies can be a challenge in your busy day-to-day life. However, by carrying some of your hobbies around with you, you can begin to experience them spontaneously. For instance, carry a book or knitting needles in your bag and make your rush-hour commute more enjoyable, or have a notebook and pen with you in case you observe something that you would like to write about or draw.

Spontaneity is also about practising flexibility. If you make plans with a friend and they fall through, remember that it's not the end of the world. Think of ways to make the most of your freed-up time. And remember, spontaneity is not simply about diving off the steepest cliff; it is about keeping an open mind to life's possibilities and actively embracing new experiences

---

169

EAT TOGETHER

Eating dinner together can have a powerful effect on family wellbeing. Research shows that children who eat more often with their family tend to have a healthier diet overall and may be less at risk of obesity and depression. Some studies show that family meals can improve social wellbeing and academic behaviour among teenagers.

It's not just the act of eating together that matters, but also the opportunity to create fun, shared experiences and the space to connect with one another in your busy lives.

170

STRAWBERRY AND CUCUMBER FACE MASK

Here is a face mask that will tone and revitalise your skin and restore its healthy colour. Antioxidants in the strawberries help to neutralise the damaging molecules known as free radicals, which may have robbed the skin of its lustre. Cucumber is very cooling, while honey is an excellent healer.

- 1 tablespoon ground almonds
- 3 strawberries
- ½ cucumber
- 1 teaspoon honey
- 1 tablespoon yoghurt

Blend the ingredients together until smooth. Apply the mixture to cleansed, damp skin. Leave for 15 minutes or until dry. Gently wipe off with a damp facecloth.

171

GORGE ON GRAPEFRUIT

Juicy and sharp, grapefruit is a great food to enjoy at the start of the day. It is a relatively recent arrival in the fruit world – having appeared about 300 years ago in the Caribbean as a result of either natural or deliberate horticultural cross-breeding – but has long been revered for its healthy properties. Grapefruit is very low in saturated fat, cholesterol and sodium. It is also a good source of dietary fibre and vitamin C, as well as containing some vitamin A. But resist the temptation to sprinkle refined sugar over it before eating as you will undo some of its nutritional goodness by increasing your intake of 'bad' carbohydrates.

DAILY INSPIRATION

'True enjoyment comes from activity of the mind and exercise of the body; the two are united.'

Alexander von Humboldt
Geographer, naturalist, explorer (1769–1859)

HEALTH DAY: PEA AND BROAD BEAN SOUP

This recipe is ideal for keeping your kidneys healthy. Peas are a good source of vitamin C, as well as supplying the iron, carotenes and B vitamins necessary for a healthy nervous system.

225g (2 cups) fresh peas
225g (1½ cups) fresh broad beans
900ml (30.5 fl oz) vegetable stock
Salt and freshly ground black pepper
8 small slices gluten-free bread
1 clove garlic, sliced lengthways
4 tablespoons olive oil
Plain probiotic yoghurt
Harissa paste

Place the peas, beans and stock in a large saucepan and bring to a boil. Cover and simmer for 30 minutes, or until the beans are tender. Pour into a food processor or blender and blend until smooth. Pour back into the pan and heat through. Season with salt and black pepper. Place the bread slices on a grill rack and rub the cut side of the clove of garlic over them. Drizzle with olive oil and toast under the grill, turning once during cooking. To serve, pour the soup into bowls, add a spoonful of yoghurt and arrange two slices of bread on top of each portion, then spoon a little harissa over each.

Serves four.

174

SPEND LESS TIME GROCERY SHOPPING

An effective way to save both time and money is by spending less time in the supermarket. A quick visit to the store to pick up a few ingredients or a ready meal may seem harmless in itself, but more often than not we end up with a basketful of items that we hadn't expected to buy.

Planning is key to cost- and time-effective grocery shopping. By drafting a basic meal plan for the week, you can see which items you have already and make a list of the items you need to buy – a task that takes less than 10 minutes. Having a list with you in the supermarket also prevents you from making impulse buys by focusing you on particular items. In addition to saving money by limiting unnecessary purchases, you will also be cutting down on wasted food and shedding hours off your weekly shop.

175

ONLY WORRY ABOUT THINGS YOU CAN CHANGE

Few things erode your mental wellbeing faster than worrying – especially about things you can't change. Some things are obviously out of your control, like world events and the weather. But there are many less obvious circumstances you can't change – including what others do, many work challenges, some economic circumstances, even personality traits you were born with.

Devote your mental energy to the things you can change and your problems will seem more manageable. And instead of worrying on your own, talk things over with a friend, or ask others for help.

176

TRAIN THE BRAIN: QUICK CONUNDRUM

A man lives on the 13th floor of a downtown block of flats. Every weekday he takes the lift to go down to the ground floor to go to work. When he returns, he takes the lift to the 8th floor and then walks up the stairs to reach his flat on the 13th floor. If it is raining, he does the same thing, except he takes the lift to the 10th floor before walking.

He hates walking, so why does he do it?

Answer: The man is very short, and cannot reach higher than the lift button for the 8th floor, except if it is raining, when he is able to use his umbrella to hit the 10th floor button.

177

SAVOUR SEAWEED

Extensive studies have shown that seaweed is a veritable superfood with incredible diet and beauty benefits. Full of protein, minerals and vitamins, seaweed is known to regulate hormones (which can, in turn, prevent diseases like breast cancer), aid digestion, rid your body of toxins and improve heart health. Seaweed is also delicious, low in calories and easy to incorporate into everyday dishes like soups, salads and stir-fries. Dried seaweed can be bought from many supermarkets, specialist stores and health food shops. So stock up – it may dramatically change your health from the inside out.

BE GRATEFUL

Practising gratefulness and developing a positive outlook go hand in hand. If you think about all of the things in your life that you have to be grateful for – like loved ones or good health – more often than not optimism naturally follows. Several studies show that gratitude can have surprising health benefits, especially for people recovering from life-threatening or long-term illnesses. According to one study, patients who saw gains and felt grateful after suffering a heart attack were less likely to experience a second heart attack.

Keeping a gratitude journal is an effective way to document the things in your life that you are thankful for. In addition to reaping the therapeutic benefits of listing things you are grateful for, the journal may help you regain perspective when times seem difficult.

Being grateful towards yourself and others will draw positive energy towards you. Openly expressing your gratitude reminds the people in your life that they are appreciated and loved. Gratitude can also strengthen relationships with loved ones, colleagues and connections. According to Harvard Medical School, couples who openly express gratitude are also more likely to express concerns about their relationship to one another.

Here are some suggestions to bolster your personal relationships:

- Tell someone that you love them.
- Thank someone who has done something for you with a handwritten note.
- Do a favour for someone without expecting something in return – just show them you're grateful to have them in your life.

HOST A PICNIC

Hosting an old-fashioned picnic party is a great excuse to get all your friends and family together to enjoy the pleasures of the great outdoors. Whether it's a company outing, family reunion or casual Saturday lunch, picnics give you valuable social bonding time with colleagues, friends and family. They can also put you and your family back in touch with nature, which will relieve stress and reduce blood pressure.

For a fun-filled, healthy afternoon picnic, fill your basket or cooler bag with these items:

- Eating utensils, including plates, cutlery, napkins, cups and/or glasses
- A range of drinks, such as water and fruit juice. You may want to include hot drinks as well, in which case, pack a flask of hot water with your favourite herbal tea.
- Sandwiches are a picnic staple. Try egg, tuna, cheese and pickle, or ham and cheese. Avoid ingredients that will make the bread soggy, or pack them in a separate container so that you can add them in just before you eat.
- A choice of dips with crudités
- A selection of fruit, such as strawberries, grapes and raspberries
- You'll also need a cosy blanket or two to sit on – plus a couple of quaint tablecloths to place over them so that they don't get dirty.
- Remember to bring a couple of rubbish bags for clearing up.

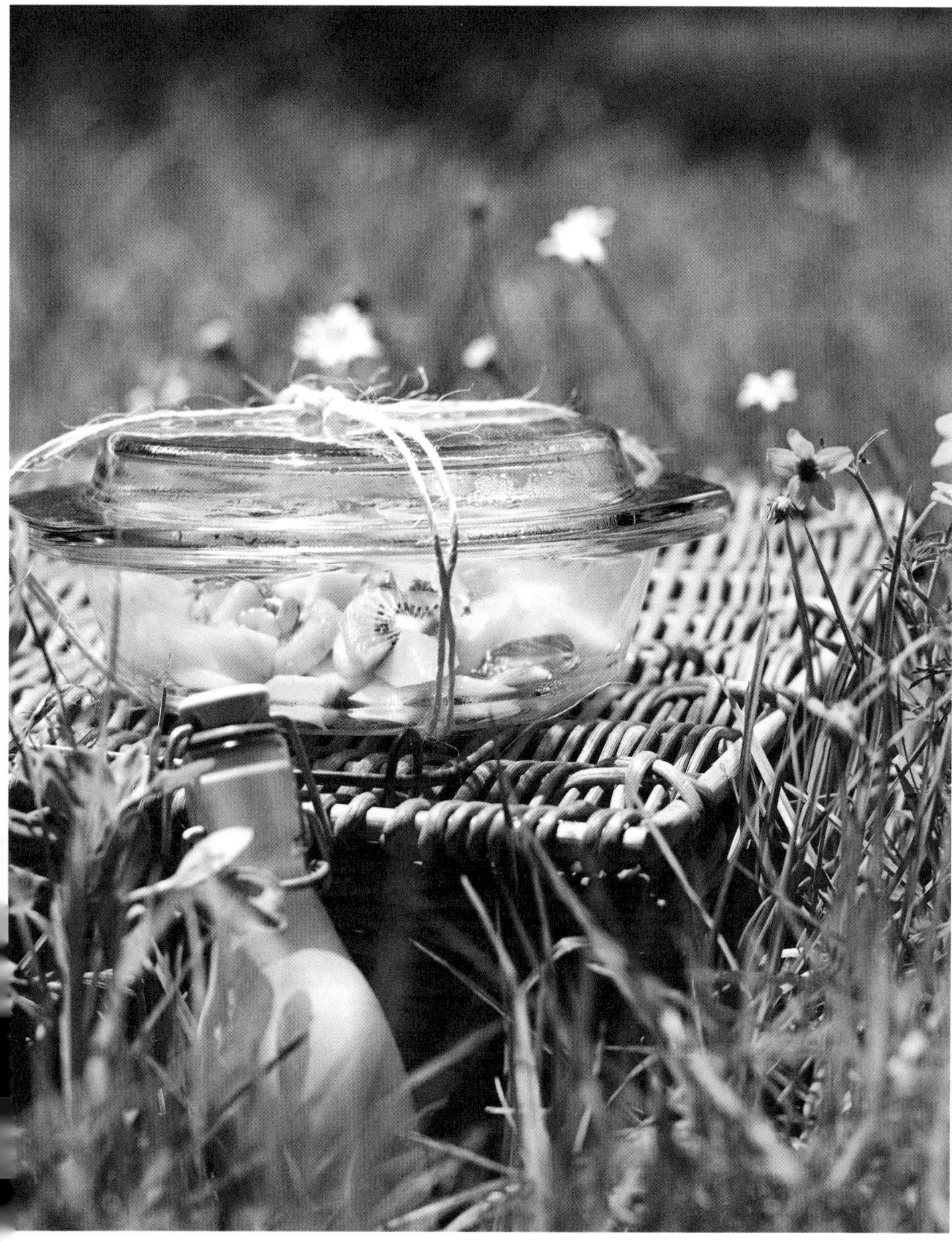

180

STRETCH: CALF MUSCLES

Calf muscles can become sore after jumping, running or even just walking. This stretch can be performed either kneeling or standing – if you want to it standing, start in a lunge position, press the back heel down as below and lean forward slightly to increase the stretch before holding and repeating.

- Position yourself on the floor on your hands and knees. Take one leg straight behind you and use it to anchor yourself onto the floor. Press the heel of your back leg away from you. You will feel a stretch in your calf muscle.
- Hold the stretch for 15 seconds, then repeat on the other leg.

181

TRY TEA-TREE OIL

An essential oil extracted from leaves of the tea-tree (not the same as the common tea plant), tea tree oil was discovered in Australia, where it was used for many centuries as an antiseptic. It has grown in popularity recently as an all-purpose skin treatment. It has been praised for its versatility and has been shown to be an effective treatment for minor skin conditions, such as spots.

If you like the camphor scent, tea-tree oil can also be used for cleaning – combine two teaspoons of tea-tree oil with two cups of water to make a general spray-cleaner, or add a few drops to your laundry for an enhanced fresh smell.

182

BECOME EMOTIONALLY INTELLIGENT

Emotional intelligence is the capacity to recognise and manage our emotions and those of others close to us. If we can identify emotional messages in the expression and tone of others, we're more likely to empathise with them. By understanding how emotions affect our thinking, we can use them for more effective problem-solving, decision-making and creative pursuits.

Finding ways to manage emotions effectively – relaxing when nervous or remaining calm when angry, for example – is the crux of emotional intelligence and can increase our chances of happiness. When you feel a bad mood coming on, there are plenty of ways to ward it off:

- Expend some energy – get some physical exercise.
- Give yourself a pep-talk – or find a friend to give you one.
- Change position – get up from your desk, look up, stretch and walk around.
- Go outside, if you can.
- Don't resort to drink, drugs or comfort food.
- Listen to some relaxing music.
- Don't avoid the person or thing that has upset you.
- Go to a yoga class.
- Meditate.
- Find a pleasant distraction, such as a hobby.
- Have a chat with a friend.

Speak Your Mind
Embrace the Value of Sleep
Eat More Alkaline
Plant Spring Bulbs
Go to the Theatre
Stop Ageing with Antioxidants
Stretch
Be a Lifelong Student
Have an Active Holiday
Make Your Bedroom a Cocoon
Health Day
Make Homemade Massage Oil
Don't Dwell
Watch a Sunset
Join an Evening Class
Bring Colour into Your Home
Have Regular Health Checks
Keep a Pet
Daily Inspiration
Try Acupuncture
Communicate at Work
Go for the Goji
Discover Bach's Flower Remedies
Train the Brain
Create a Daily Ritual
Seek Responsibility at Work
Be Giving
Feed Your Hair
Purify Your Air with Plants
Health Day
DIY Manicure

Retreat to Your Home
Move More at Work
Watch Your Carbon Footprint
Sharpen Your Brain with Neurobics
Stretch
Eat Iron
Make Rose Water
Have a Staycation
Just Say No
Get Vaccinated
Enjoy Sex
Daily Inspiration
Take Yourself Less Seriously
Sparkle with Spinach
Trust Your Neighbours
Smile Every Day
Live with Purpose
Train the Brain
Get to a Gallery
Love Lavender
Revitalise with a Bath
Get the Royal Treatment
Expand your Vocabulary
Practise Self-Discipline
Launch a Blog
Be a Musician
Eat Your Five a Day
Health Day
Go with Your Gut
Try New Activities with Your Partner
Discover Family History

Daydream
Daily Inspiration
Join a Sports Team
Recycle to Help the Planet
Make a Scrapbook
Switch off the TV
Find an Exercise Buddy
Relax and Unwind
Thirsty Skin Moisturiser
Get Up an Hour Earlier
Skip a Meal
Believe You Can Do Better
Walk the Path to Better Thinking
Grow Roses
Brush Up Every Day
Health Day
Manage Your Time
Lose the Fear
Send Snail Mail
Love What Your Do
Stretch
Improve Your Spatial Skills
Daily Inspiration
Train the Brain
Keep Thoughts for Others
Maintain a Healthy Bank Balance
Personalise Gifts
Go Green with Tea
Juice Day

AUTUMN

The cooler weather is ideal for exercising, reconnecting with the outdoors and rediscovering the garden. Try acupuncture, royal jelly or brain training to keep you in blooming health through the colder seasons. Focus on nurturing your body and bolstering your immune system before winter arrives.

SPEAK YOUR MIND

Open communication is vitally important to any relationship. By acknowledging and communicating your feelings, you can neutralise negative emotions and limit the stress that comes with those feelings.

When speaking our minds honestly and openly, we are able to deal directly with the problems that are bothering us. Once something has been acknowledged, even if just by you, the problem sometimes seems to fade away or lose its former importance. Bottling your feelings puts you at risk of exploding later on, and it can have a direct effect on the people around you. If you decide to hold a grudge or give someone the silent treatment, you may be inadvertently causing hurt or breeding more conflict.

If you are finding it particularly difficult to voice your opinion or express your feelings, remember these points:

- Do not be afraid of how others may react. Remember that your opinions and feelings are just as important as everyone else's.
- Think rationally about what you want to say and communicate your feelings clearly and respectfully. People usually don't react well to being yelled at; it can make them feel hurt or defensive.
- Try to keep a calm state of mind when explaining why something is bothering you. If the person you're speaking to values your feelings, they will most likely listen.

EMBRACE THE VALUE OF SLEEP

Research has consistently shown that people who suffer from insomnia experience lower feelings of both psychological and subjective wellbeing, while people who sleep an average of six to eight and a half hours per night report the best levels of psychological and subjective wellbeing. They report fewer symptoms of depression and anxiety, more positive relationships with others, plus greater levels of control and purpose in their lives.

The causes of insomnia are well established; for example, coffee, smoking or taking drugs, stress, depression and anxiety as well as factors such as the bedroom being too hot or too noisy. Luckily the things that you can do to improve your chances of having a good night's sleep are also well researched.

- Stick to a regular sleep schedule, with the same bedtime every night, and a regular relaxing routine to help you wind down.
- Avoid late-night stimulants such as coffee (even decaffeinated), tea, hot chocolate and alcohol. Try herbal teas, especially chamomile, or milk instead.
- When lying in bed, don't focus on what went wrong during the day.
- If you can't get to sleep after 20 minutes in bed, get up and sit quietly for a while before trying again. Don't watch TV or put on bright lights as this will tell your brain it's time to wake up.
- Some resting yoga positions, such as Child's Pose or Corpse Pose, are known to relax the body, calm the mind and combat restlessness. Practise for 10 minutes before going to bed.

185

EAT MORE ALKALINE

By switching to a more plant-based diet that is high in vegetables and fruits and lower in protein, you can improve your overall health as well as having a positive impact on the environment. Vegetables and fruits are generally classified as 'alkaline' – meaning that they have an alkalising effect on the body's pH balance – whereas protein-based foods such as meat, fish and beans are classified as 'acidic'. If the body's pH consistently registers towards the acidic end of the scale, a whole host of health problems results. However, by simply cutting back on your protein consumption by at least 60 per cent, you can greatly reduce your risk of cancer, diabetes, heart disease and death.

Cutting back on meat consumption can have a significant impact on the environment's health as well. According to the charity WWF (formerly the World Wildlife Fund), people in Britain need to cut their meat consumption by 75 per cent to reach climate-change targets. According to the UN Food and Agriculture Organization, meat production generates about 18 per cent of the world's greenhouse-gas emissions – more than the total for transport.

Eating more alkaline is easy to do:

- At mealtimes, aim for a good alkaline–acid balance. The ratio should ideally be two parts alkaline foods to one part acidic foods.
- Instate 'meat-free' days during the week where you cook only vegetarian or vegan meals.
- Meat quality makes a huge difference when it comes to your health and environment. Instead of supermarket cuts that likely come from factory farms, favour vendors who sell organic, locally sourced and sustainable meats.

186

PLANT SPRING BULBS

There is nothing more likely to lift your spirits after a long winter than sprouted spring bulbs. Daffodils, winter aconites, tulips, grape hyacinths and other bulbs are among the easiest plants to grow, needing only well-drained soil and some sunshine. Planting drifts of bulbs in a border will help to fill in the gaps and provide colour before perennials and shrubs begin to grow in early spring.

If you want a colourful patio or window-ledge display, try growing bulbs in pots. Fill with compost mixed with a handful of horticultural grit, plant the bulbs and water. Keep the compost moist and protect the pot from frost by wrapping in bubblewrap over winter.

187

GO TO THE THEATRE

Seeing a live theatre performance is an emotive and uplifting experience. You become more involved and invested in the story and characters because you are immersed in the action on stage. The theatre is also a great way to escape the stresses of life for an evening and will give you something to look forward to.

The iconic national and international music and theatre shows are great, but don't forget the local scene. Bars and other small, independent venues offer a fantastic way to discover new talent and tickets are often much cheaper. You can also feel good about attending local performances because they allow you to contribute to your community's art scene in a more direct manner.

STOP AGEING WITH ANTIOXIDANTS

One of the main theories about why the body degenerates as you grow older is based on a chemical process known as oxidation. During normal metabolism the body produces unstable molecules called free radicals, but there are other factors in the environment that also increase free-radical production.

Fortunately, you have a supply of natural antidotes called antioxidants, which mop up free radicals. However, levels of antioxidants fall as you age, resulting in damage to cells and tissues. By increasing your intake of antioxidants as you get older, you may be able to protect yourself from the worst effects of this process. A wide range of chemicals in food can act as antioxidants, but among the most important are beta-carotene and the vitamins A, C and E. Research on people who follow a diet rich in antioxidants, rather than relying on supplements, has been promising, for example in reducing the risk of Alzheimer's disease.

Foods that are rich in antioxidants:

- Beans: pinto, red, black and kidney beans
- Berries: cranberries, blueberries and blackberries
- Nuts: pecans, walnuts and hazelnuts
- Other fruits: plums, cherries, apples
- Artichoke hearts
- Russet potatoes.

189

STRETCH: SHOULDERS

Your shoulders can become tired through prolonged or repetitive movements, such as sitting at a desk for long periods. This is an easy stretch that can be done anywhere, helping to improve posture and reduce muscle tension.

- Stand a little away from a wall. Place your hands on the wall and walk your feet away until your upper body is horizontal, with back and arms straight and hands still pressing on the wall.
- Press your armpits towards the floor to feel a flexing in the shoulder joints. Press and release a few times to extend the range of movement of the shoulders.

190

BE A LIFELONG STUDENT

Intellectual activity is as important to a long and happy life as remaining physically fit and active. Continuing to learn provides new knowledge, promotes intellectual stimulation and increases satisfaction. It can also boost your enjoyment of life, your self-confidence and your ability to cope with everyday challenges.

- Take up a new hobby that requires new skills and learning.
- Go back to school or enrol in a course: it's never too late to continue your education with a university degree or master's course.
- Rather than a fictional film, watch a documentary.

191

HAVE AN ACTIVE HOLIDAY

Lazing poolside with a cocktail or two might sound like the ideal holiday when you're stressed and need a break. But is it really what you're looking for?

Especially if you lead a sedentary lifestyle, your body may be crying out for activity and your brain may need more of a challenge. An active holiday can inspire feelings of renewed health and vitality and better lifestyle choices when you return to normal life.

Consider cycling through Vietnam, camping in the wilderness or attending a health retreat with yoga and t'ai chi. It's even better if you can learn a new sport or skill while you're away. You'll gain a sense of achievement and new skills to take home that are better than any souvenir.

192

MAKE YOUR BEDROOM A COCOON

Just as cocoons are crucial for transforming insect pupae, the atmosphere in your bedroom is crucial for transforming you during sleep. Aim to make your bedroom a place of tranquillity, free from the noises and distractions of the outside world. Consider keeping the décor minimalist and, when deciding on a paint colour for your bedroom, choose soothing, cool-spectrum colours. Do not place electronics like televisions or computers in your bedroom. They are distracting and their electromagnetic fields can keep you awake and feeling irritable.

HEALTH DAY: VEGETABLE BROTH

This broth is a great-tasting regular meal for a nutritious approach to eating. It is easy to make and can also be used as a stock for other, more substantial soups.

- 4l (16 cups) cold water
- 300g (10.5 oz) organic celery
- 300g (10.5 oz) organic carrots
- 300g (10.5 oz) organic parsnips
- 100g (3.5 oz) organic potatoes
- 100g (4 cups) organic fresh mixed herbs: basil, marjoram, fennel and parsley
- Caraway, ground nutmeg, juniper berries and rock salt (to taste)

Wash all the vegetables, and grate them in a food processor. Place all vegetables in a large saucepan. Add the cold water, fresh herbs and rock salt. Simmer gently for 45 minutes. Pour the broth through a fine sieve or strainer. Reserve the liquid and discard the vegetables. Add nutmeg, juniper and caraway, and season with rock salt.

The broth will keep well for a couple of days in the fridge.

194

MAKE HOMEMADE MASSAGE OIL

Massage oils are a wonderful way to bring the healing benefits of essential oils and aromatherapy into your life.

To make a massage oil, first decide which scents soothe or invigorate you – do you prefer light and floral or zesty and fruity fragrances? Once you have made your choice, combine the oil(s) with a carrier oil such as sweet almond or rosehip oil. Read the recommendations on the carrier bottle since the recommended ratio of essential oil to carrier varies. If storing your massage blend for future use, do so in a dark glass bottle away from direct heat or sunlight.

195

DON'T DWELL

Dwelling is something we often can't resist doing, yet it can anchor us in the past and keep us from moving on. Change is normal, and even if we've already invested time and emotion in something that doesn't mean we should cling onto it indefinitely. It is helpful to think about where and why things went wrong, but only if this knowledge is used constructively. Consider the past, but keep your mind-set facing forward. Try to accept when things have reached their conclusion and are beyond your control; and use that knowledge to flavour your understanding of new situations.

196

WATCH A SUNSET

Few things can boost your sense of wellbeing as surely as watching a sunset. Don't save this magical experience for holidays in exotic locations, make it part of your regular routine whenever you can. At its simplest, getting outside at the end of the day is good for your overall health and keeps you active. It's also incredibly relaxing, helping the mind to switch off from the day's concerns and prepare for the evening. Practise being mindful, slow down your thinking and become aware of the present moment.

If you're having trouble sleeping, even a 10-minute walk as the sun is setting can enhance secretion of the hormone melatonin and regulate the sleep–wake cycle in the sleep centre of the brain. New scientific research suggests melatonin may even guard the brain from neurodegenerative diseases like Alzheimer's.

197

JOIN AN EVENING CLASS

Taking an evening class after work offers many rewards. You will benefit from the fulfilment and sense of achievement that can accompany learning a new skill. It can also be a different and fun way to socialise with friends or make new ones. And being busy in the evening with something you enjoy will take your mind off work and other life stresses, inspiring and invigorating you.

If you love the arts, try life drawing, painting, sculpting, pottery, photography, acting or creative writing. If you want to move, sign up for dancing classes or self-defence. Learn a musical instrument such as piano, guitar or flute or join a choir. Your choices are endless.

BRING COLOUR INTO YOUR HOME

The colours you introduce to your home can have an impact on your wellbeing, since different colours are known to influence different emotions. And it is not just the colours that you use, but where you use them in the home, and how. When making your choice for a room, you may wish to consider the main emotional impact that specific colours are meant to have.

You can use just one main colour throughout a room, or different tones of the same colour. Alternatively, you can place extra splashes of 'accent' colour(s) – to complement a dominant colour, or even equal amounts of two or more contrasting colours, making sure that there are no uneasy clashes. Objects that you should consider when matching or introducing a colour scheme are soft furnishings (cushions, rugs, bedding); ornaments (framed photos, lamps, vases, sculptures); kitchenware (toaster, fruit bowls, tea towels); tableware (tablecloths, place mats, crockery) and floral arrangements, with endless colour options.

Here are some common colours and their associations:

Red: Fiery and invigorating

Orange: Warm and reassuring

Green: Nourishing and soothing

Blue: Calming and cooling

Yellow: Sunny and uplifting

Brown: Grounding and practical.

199

HAVE REGULAR HEALTH CHECKS

The earlier you identify a disease the less damage it is likely to do and the easier it should be to treat. Be vigilant for odd lumps and bumps, strange pains, rashes or other changes in your body – and get medical advice about anything that worries you. But, mostly, the only way to pick up the first stages of a condition is through regular screening, even if you're an ostensibly healthy person.

Screening is available for many serious diseases, but it can cause a lot of unnecessary worry. Ask your doctor about the efficacy of tests and how often they should be repeated.

200

KEEP A PET

Pet ownership can have a good effect on your blood pressure and heart rate and potentially reduce the incidence of stress and depression. In one study comparing people who owned a dog or a cat with people who did not, participants were required to complete mental arithmetic tests. Pet owners who took the tests in the presence of their pets exhibited lower heart rate and blood pressure, and recovered faster afterwards. Also, taking your dog for regular walks brings you into contact with other dog owners, allowing you to connect with others.

DAILY INSPIRATION

'We are what we repeatedly do. Excellence, therefore, is not an act but a habit.'

Aristotle
Greek philosopher (384 – 322 BCE)

TRY ACUPUNCTURE

Nowadays, acupuncture is increasingly recommended as a complementary therapy by professionals trained in Western medicine.

The principle of acupuncture is that when needles are inserted into specific points on the body it stimulates the flow of 'Qi' or energy. When this energy is stagnant or overactive, it is thought to cause fatigue, discomfort and disease.

Worldwide, there is still debate about the therapeutic effects of this ancient practice. However in 2003, the World Health Organization (WHO) published a review and analysis of controlled clinical trials that listed 28 conditions for which 'acupuncture has been proved – through controlled trials – to be an effective treatment'.

Many people swear by acupuncture to relieve the following conditions:

- Stress
- Sports injuries, such as tennis elbow
- Chronic pain, carpal tunnel syndrome and osteoarthritis
- Digestive complaints, such as nausea and vomiting
- Women's health issues, such as menstrual cramps, infertility and menopause.

If you suffer from any of the above, consider asking your doctor about acupuncture.

203

COMMUNICATE AT WORK

Communication is an art form. It can be a powerful tool for getting through life and has a great impact on our personal and professional relationships. Expressing yourself or relaying a message with sensitivity, honesty, respect and professionalism is a fantastic way to build positive relationships. But different people and situations require different approaches.

You will probably meet people with vastly different characters, from vastly different backgrounds during your career. Sensitivity and respect are the key words here to keeping it professional. Pay attention to the type of person you are meeting and engage accordingly. Stay calm even if adverse exchanges occur. If possible, be prepared: know your conversation topic, your company policies and the background of the person you are meeting. Don't divulge too much personal information upon first meeting – keep things brief and clear.

204

GO FOR THE GOJI

Goji berries are full of vitamins, particularly vitamin A and vitamin C, are a good source of calcium and fibre and contain more iron than steak. Goji berries are also full of compounds called phytochemicals – natural chemicals, including flavonoids, tannins and carotenoids – which have important health benefits. Dried goji berries can be eaten raw or cooked. With a taste similar to raisins, and slightly crunchy in texture, they are good sprinkled on breakfast cereals or added to fruit salads.

205

TRAIN THE BRAIN: MIND TEASERS

Expand your mental capacity and consider new ways of thinking with these logic puzzles and mind-bending problems.

1: Two boys are born to the same mother, on the same day, at the same time, in the same year and yet they're not twins. How can this be?

2: On what seems to be a normal evening, Ted and Alice are sitting together in their front room. Ted is watching DVDs, while Alice is reading a book. Suddenly, for no apparent reason, the power goes out. Ted curses, and then decides to go to bed. But Alice declines to follow him. With no use of artificial light, and in the pitch-dark, she keeps on reading. How?

Answers: 1. The two boys are two of a set of triplets. 2. Alice is blind and reading a Braille book.

206

CREATE A DAILY RITUAL

Daily rituals can provide a sense of comfort, ease and purpose. A ritual doesn't have to be something amazing or unique, just something that you can try to do every day that will reset your mind and gear you up for the day's challenges. It may be a connection to the physical, intellectual or spiritual part of your life, but the important thing is that it acknowledges what you consider to be important. No two daily rituals are the same so do whatever works for you.

DISCOVER BACH'S FLOWER REMEDIES

Towards the end of the nineteenth century, English physician Dr Edward Bach developed a theory for treating a patient's emotional state using flower remedies. Such theories had first been put into practice by the Swiss healer Paracelsus in the 1500s.

You take flower essences by dotting them onto your tongue or by drinking a few drops in a glass of water. The idea is that they help you to deal with a number of emotional conditions – shock, jealousy, hatred and intolerance, for example – and work by stimulating the body's own capacity to heal itself by balancing negative feelings. The remedies can be useful in helping you to take control of a situation, to kick-start your motivation or to break a bad habit.

Although specific emotional conditions are associated with certain flowers, it is best to visit a registered healer rather than to prescribe the remedies for yourself. He or she will either make you a bespoke remedy or recommend an all-encompassing blend. Here is a list of emotions and their corresponding flower remedies:

Happiness: Willow, crab apple, sweet chestnut, wild rose, olive, elm, larch, mustard, oak, honeysuckle, white chestnut, star of Bethlehem, pine and clematis

Fears: Red chestnut, rock rose, mimulus, aspen, cherry plum, chestnut bud

Self-assurance: Wild oat, hornbeam, holly, walnut, centaury, agrimony, gorse, gentian, cerato and scleranthus

Acceptance: Vervain, chicory, water violet, heather, vine, rock water, beech and impatiens.

208

SEEK RESPONSIBILITY AT WORK

Rather than salary or status, the most important factors behind job satisfaction are how much control employees have over the type of work they do and how meaningful their jobs are. Even though stress tends to increase as people rise through the ranks, so too does autonomy – and it is this, or the lack of it, that affects wellbeing and satisfaction at work.

So whenever possible, seek out more responsibility at work – not only could it improve your chances of career progression by showing initiative, the increased autonomy will also lead to greater job satisfaction.

209

BE GIVING

All of us have items that we've kept in our lives for their sentimental value, items that were given to us at some point and were once of use or things that have simply managed to avoid all the usual clear-outs and have lain gathering dust for years. Donating to your local charity shops provides an excellent excuse to clear out your wardrobe while contributing to a good cause. Whether it's that top you once loved, or that book that you obsessed over during your teens, it's nice to think that someone else can get the same joy again from that item. Not only are you helping yourself to move forward and organise your life, but others along the way can gain something from your actions, too.

210

FEED YOUR HAIR

What we eat can have an effect on all areas of our bodies, and that includes the appearance of our hair. So if your locks are looking lacklustre, consider adding the following to your diet:

- Pumpkin seeds add shine to your hair. They're also a good source of iron, which supplies oxygen to the hair roots, makes hair grow faster and prevents hair loss. Pumpkin seeds also contain protein, which is crucial to the production of keratin, the hair's protective coating, and zinc, which strengthens hair follicles.
- Walnuts can help if your hair colour is fading. They contain copper, which is needed by the body to produce melanin pigments. Melanin gives hair its colour, and it also helps to thicken and add shine to the hair. Eating walnuts may also help to reverse the greying of hair.

211

PURIFY YOUR AIR WITH PLANTS

Whether you're eating them or scattering them through your house, plants give life around every corner. They turn carbon dioxide into oxygen during the day and purify the air by soaking up damaging free radicals. Some beautifully coloured flowers brighten a room and can lift your mood. Place a few flowers or plants in the kitchen, dining room or lounge.

To keep tulips and other cut flowers fresher for longer, add liquid plant food and change their water regularly.

HEALTH DAY: PEAR AND PUMPKIN STEW

Among a wide ranges of minerals – iron, thiamine, calcium, potassium – pears contain 15 per cent of the daily recommended amount of vitamin C. And being packed full of fibre, they give your stomach the impression of being full, which also means you're less likely to overindulge.

- 2 cloves garlic, peeled and crushed
- 115g (4 oz) bread
- 3 tablespoons olive oil
- 55g (¾ cup) ground almonds
- 1 teaspoon paprika
- 1 onion, chopped
- 125ml (½ cup) dry white wine
- 115g (4 oz) carrots, peeled and sliced
- 115g (4 oz) pumpkin or squash, peeled and cubed
- 4 firm pears, cored and cubed
- 1 x 400g (14 oz) can chopped tomatoes
- Few strands saffron
- 225g (1⅓ cup) cooked or tinned chickpeas, rinsed

Preheat the oven to 220°C. Slice the bread thickly and brush with one tablespoon of olive oil and crushed garlic. Arrange on a baking tray and bake until golden. Leave to cool, then break the bread into pieces. Blend in a food processor with the almonds and paprika.

Fry the onion in the remaining olive oil in a large saucepan until soft. Add the wine and 750ml (1⅓ pint) of water. Bring to the boil. Add the carrots, pumpkin and pear to the saucepan along with the tomatoes and saffron and simmer for 15 minutes until the vegetables are tender. Stir in the bread paste and the chickpeas, and reheat before serving.

Serves four.

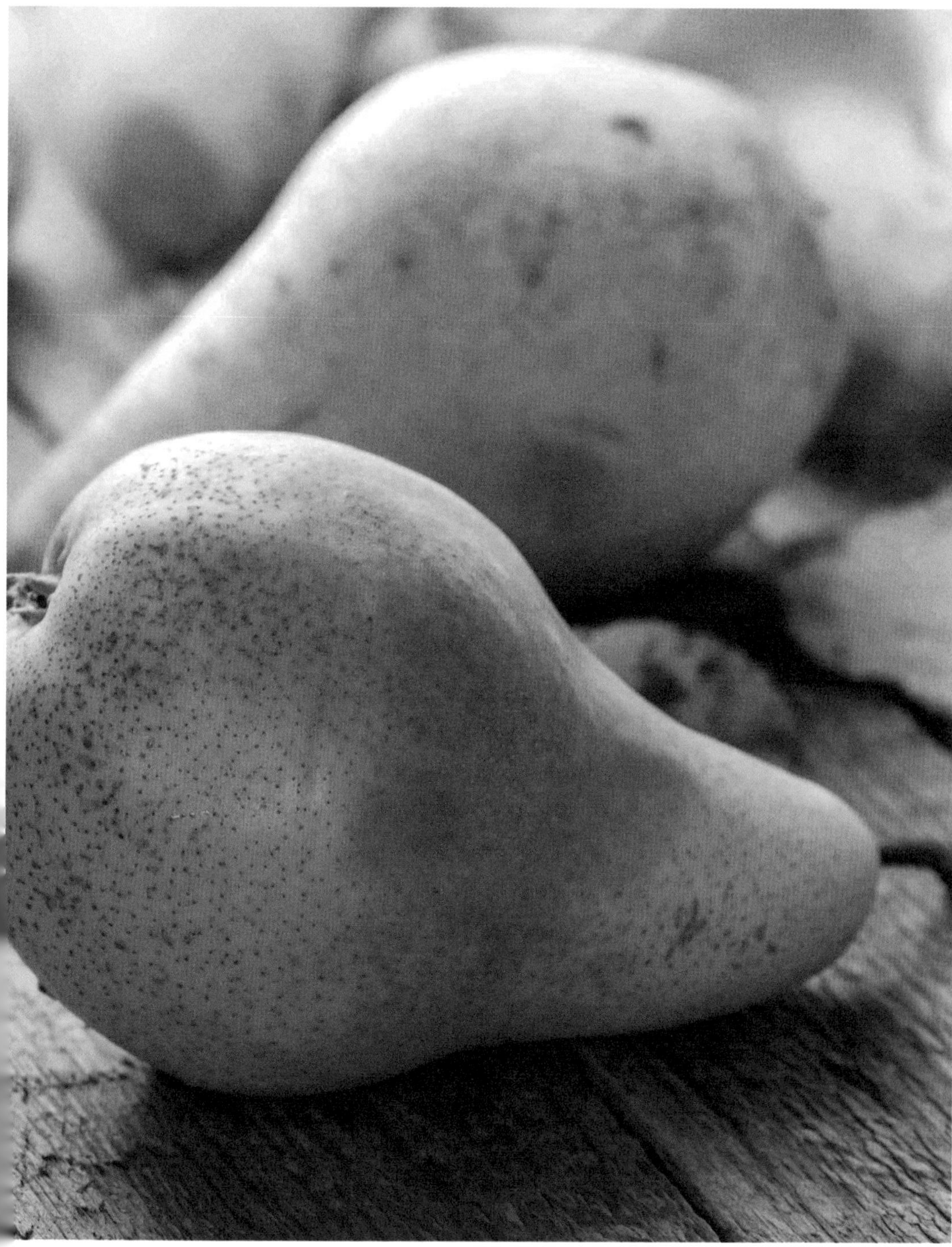

213

DIY MANICURE

It is all too easy to forget about your hands – and before you know it you are faced with rough skin and chipped, uneven nails. Here are some simple tips for keeping your hands flawless:

- Wear gloves whenever possible, particularly when putting your hands in water.
- When exfoliating your face, rub any remaining product into the backs of your hands. This removes any dead skin, revealing soft new skin underneath.
- Trim your nails every two to three weeks using nail clippers rather than scissors. File your nails in one direction rather than using a seesaw action.
- Apply a rich hand cream to moisturise the skin and cuticles after washing your hands.

214

RETREAT TO YOUR HOME

A retreat is an investment in your wellbeing that can pay off for months to come. By taking the time to escape from the noise of everyday life, you are giving yourself permission to relax fully and deeply. The effects can be profound: boosted immune system and a refreshed state of mind.

You don't have to go somewhere exotic or expensive to retreat. With a little planning, it's easy to create a wellness sanctuary in your own home. Stock the pantry with healthy foods for a few days, stay inside and don't answer the phone. Gently meditate, stretch, read, rest, contemplate – whatever nourishes your mind and body and rejuvenates you for the coming months.

215

MOVE MORE AT WORK

Looking after your body is just as important during working hours as it is during your free time. Yet most of us spend far too many hours sitting still in the workplace. Research into the health outcomes of sedentary behaviour suggests that sitting in front of a computer all day can contribute to a range of chronic illnesses such as type-2 diabetes. It can also lead to more mundane complaints like muscle stiffness and joint pain.

Your body is made to move, so at the very least, change your position or posture frequently. Using a sit-stand desk is an excellent way to reposition the body and redistribute weight, which can reduce musculoskeletal pain and stress on the body. Activities like stretching and moving around regularly, taking the stairs and walking at lunchtime should be part of your daily routine.

216

WATCH YOUR CARBON FOOTPRINT

If you want to shrink your carbon footprint, start with an energy audit on your home. You can either do this yourself, by checking whether you are spending more on your utility bills than you should be, or have it done by professionals. Most utility providers will do an audit free of charge, using specialist equipment to pinpoint how your house is losing heat, for example. Once the survey has been completed, you will still need to implement their suggestions before you start making energy savings. But at least you'll know how you can make a difference.

SHARPEN YOUR BRAIN WITH NEUROBICS

Neurobics is the science of brain exercise based on the latest neuroscience research. New evidence shows that giving your brain a workout as well as your body helps stave off age-related cognitive decline. We generate new brain cells and new connections between them throughout life, meaning we can build up mental reserves by enhancing our cognitive abilities.

The good news is, it's relatively easy to strengthen memory and attention, as well as improve our mental agility, problem-solving and visuo-spatial skills. Mental stimulation is the key – the more we challenge our brains, the more new neural pathways are formed.

Introducing novelty is vital, whether it's learning something completely new, or doing familiar things, but differently. It doesn't have to be complicated for your brain to benefit, just new. Try some of the following:

- Use your non-dominant hand for everyday tasks.
- Challenge your grey matter with online brain training.
- Play board, word and card games that require you to strategise.
- Take a shower or eat with your eyes closed.
- Don't rely too heavily on technology – remember or work out information for yourself if you can.

218

STRETCH: FORWARD BEND POSE

Forward bends give an excellent stretch to the whole of the back of the body. They tone the abdominal organs and the kidneys, improving digestion and circulation.

- Start seated with your legs straight out in front of you and your feet hip-width apart and bend forward over your legs.
- You may find this pose difficult to begin with so try looping a strap around your feet to help you to hold it.
- If you can, hook your big toes with your index finger.
- Do not bounce in the pose and take extra care if you have back problems or sciatica.

219

EAT IRON

Iron deficiency is the most widespread nutritional problem in the world. Some 30 per cent of the world's population is anaemic, and about half the cases are attributable to iron deficiency. Among the many consequences of anaemia are low physical endurance, impaired immune response and poor intellectual performance.

The good news is that supplements are very effective in treating iron deficiency, and there are many high-iron foods that you can incorporate into your diet, such as lamb, beef, kidney beans, lentils, dried figs and quinoa.

MAKE ROSE WATER

Rose water has a subtle fragrance that can be nostalgic for many of us. The smell is at once musky and sweet. Rose water is made very simply and can be used in cooking or as a cosmetic. Middle Eastern cuisine features rose water in baklava and Turkish delight – a hint of the exotic when combined with pistachio nuts, as it often is. In India, rose water is dropped into the eyes to clear them. Cosmetically, pure rose water has antiseptic properties and, when applied directly, can soothe irritated skin.

Fresh rose petals, washed
Water
Ice cubes

Place something heavy, such as a Pyrex loaf dish, upside down in the centre of a large pot as a pedestal, and place a heatproof glass bowl on top of it.

Add the rose petals to the pot, placing them around the loaf dish and almost to the same depth. Add just enough water to cover them. If the lid of your pot is rounded, place it upside down so that it's inverted; otherwise, place a stainless-steel bowl on top of the pan. The lid needs to be large enough to seal the pot but shallow enough that its bottom does not touch the heatproof glass bowl. Turn up the heat to bring the water to the boil.

Add the ice cubes into the inverted lid: as the rose-infused steam rising from the water hits the underside of the cold lid, it will condense and drop into the internal bowl.

Turn the heat down to a simmer and leave for two to four hours. Every now and again, carefully lift the lid and take out a little rose water, stopping when the rose scent of the liquid begins to weaken. Replace the ice and the boiling water if need be; do not let the water boil dry.

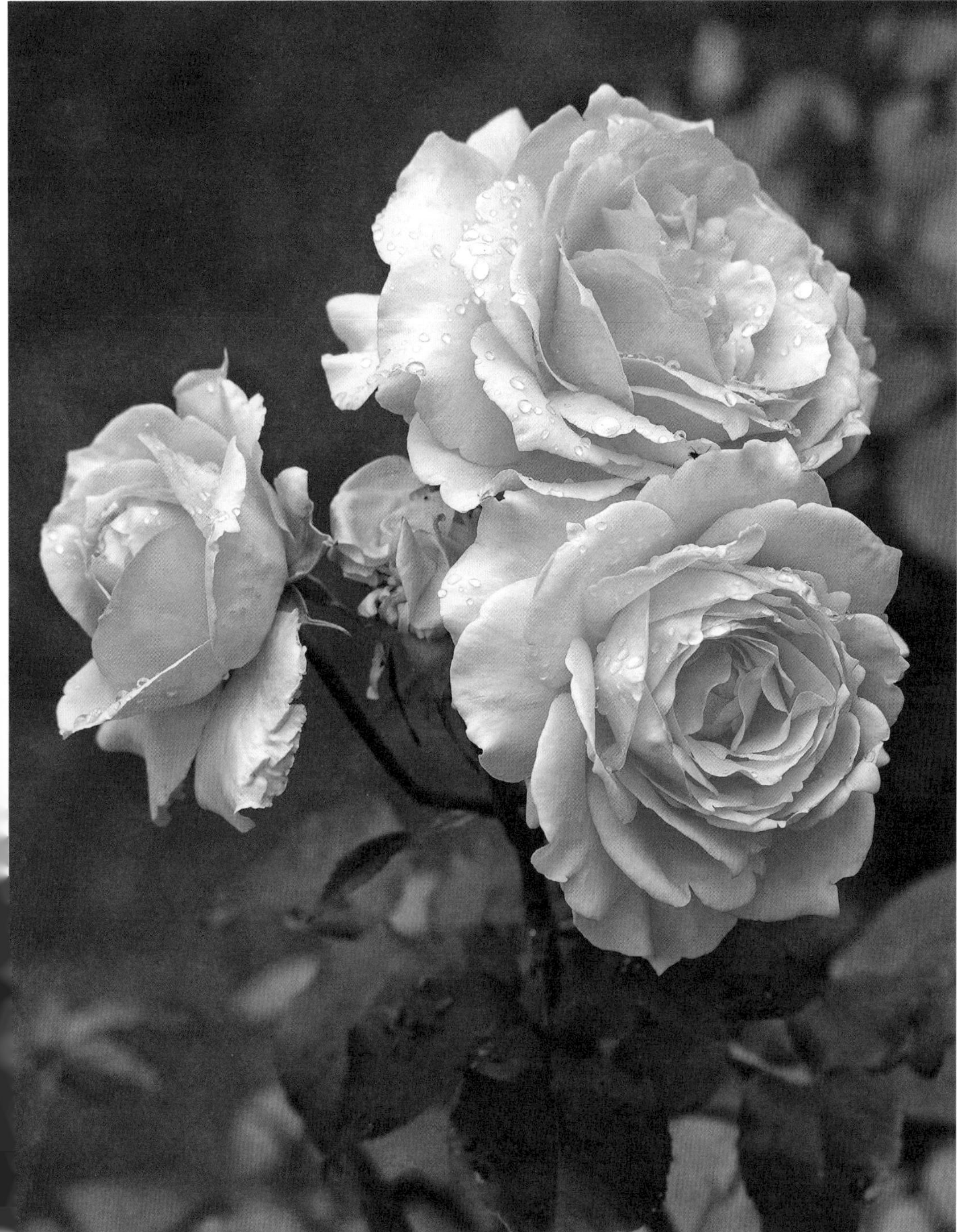

221

HAVE A STAYCATION

Holidays are great opportunities to visit different cities or countries but more often than not we ignore the communities that we live in. Instead of paying hundreds or even thousands of pounds for an exotic trip, consider taking a 'staycation'.

On your staycation, you can explore the parts of your community that you've never been to before. Try a new restaurant, visit local art galleries and museums or have a picnic in the park – hopefully by the end you will be looking at your hometown with a refreshed perspective.

Staycations are also a wonderful chance to catch up on housework or personal admin. They allow you to relax and enjoy yourself in a familiar setting, without the added pressure of booking hotels, catching flights or adapting to new time zones.

222

JUST SAY NO

N.O. These two little letters can make a big difference to your quality of life. Learning to say 'no' to others means setting personal boundaries that are essential for wellbeing. When you recognise your limits, you are not being selfish, you are honouring yourself and your needs and you are not leaving yourself open or vulnerable to exhaustion and eventual burnout.

Next time someone asks you to bake some cakes or join yet another committee when you already have too much on the go, try saying no. It will stop you from over-committing and give you time to relax and balance out your own life.

223

GET VACCINATED

If you haven't had the standard childhood vaccinations against diseases such as measles, mumps, diphtheria, whooping cough (pertussis) and poliomyelitis, talk to your doctor about which ones you might need. Adults may be as vulnerable as children to the consequences of these infections – in fact, some of them cause more severe illness if caught in adult life. Adults need a tetanus vaccination, for example, just as much as children do, and should have a booster dose every 10 years. This disease is found all over the world and can be fatal in up to 20 per cent of cases.

International travellers also need to make sure they are fully vaccinated against infections that are prevalent in the countries they are visiting. Everyone over the age of 65 and adults with chronic disease should be vaccinated against pneumonia and influenza.

224

ENJOY SEX

We all know that sex makes us feel good in the short term but it can have a number of long-term physical and psychological benefits as well. It improves your respiratory, immune and cardiovascular systems, as well as developing strength and flexibility. Studies suggest that sex is also a key part of creating and maintaining positive human relationships because it fulfils important and basic psychological needs. For instance, being intimate, desired and respected satisfies the need to feel close to other people. Also, partners who can talk to each other openly about their sexual desires and agree on what they do in bed are satisfied in their need to feel that their activities are self-chosen and self-endorsed.

DAILY INSPIRATION

‘Those who are not looking for happiness are the most likely to find it, because those who are searching forget that the surest way to be happy is to seek happiness for others.’

Martin Luther King Jr
American civil rights activist (1929–1968)

226

TAKE YOURSELF LESS SERIOUSLY

Do you have a tendency to take yourself too seriously? We are all unique, but at the same time, we are no more or less important than anyone else.

When we focus too much on ourselves, it prevents us from connecting with the feelings and concerns of others around us. It can turn us into social outcasts and worse still, we can end up feeling superior, inferior or perfectionistic. None of these are good for our mental wellbeing.

Our happiness levels skyrocket when we can be amused by our faults, mistakes and failures and see them as opportunities to learn. With a light spirit and a playful attitude to life, we're free to shine using our own personal talents.

227

SPARKLE WITH SPINACH

As well as being almost fat-free, spinach is so low in calories that there is no point measuring a portion size. But spinach is not an 'empty' food. Like other leafy green vegetables, it is an excellent source of vitamins and minerals. A 100 gram (3.5 ounce) serving contains more than the recommended daily amount of vitamin A and nearly half the vitamin C requirement, as well as vitamins E, K, B6 and thiamin, calcium, iron, magnesium, potassium, copper and manganese.

Spinach is best eaten soon after it has been picked, since the nutritional value decreases with storage.

TRUST YOUR NEIGHBOURS

We would not have survived as a species without the ability to live and work in groups, giving each other support in times of need and sharing in times of plenty. Even today, the cohesiveness of the community we live in plays a vital role in our happiness – and one of the most important measures of that cohesiveness is trust in others.

The proportion of respondents to a World Values Survey who said that most people can be trusted ranges from seven per cent of people in Turkey to about 66 per cent in Denmark – thus indicating why Denmark often comes out at the top or near the top in international wellbeing surveys.

A study at the University of British Columbia concluded that by finding ways to build more trust in society – between the young and the old or between different ethnic groups, for example – we could increase our happiness at the same time.

Here are ways to help build trust and relations in your community:

- Take an interest and participate in community activities, or even help to organise or suggest new ones.
- Get to know your neighbours: resolve any disputes that may have occurred in the past, and consider mutually beneficial arrangements such as carpooling.
- Attend any local meetings to discuss issues that affect your area and community.

229

SMILE EVERY DAY

How often do you smile every day? Recent research has confirmed what Darwin suggested in the 1870s – that, whether you're furrowing your brow or giving a big grin, showing your emotions physically intensifies them, so smiling can actually increase your sense of wellbeing.

In experiments that involved holding a pencil in the mouth to simulate a smile or a frown, scientists have shown that a genuine smile does indeed contribute to feeling happier. It's what's known as 'facial feedback'. So, if you physically mimic a smile or a frown, your brain can be tricked into believing that you're actually feeling a positive or negative emotion, with the result that you feel that emotion in reality. But it's no good smiling half-heartedly – your smile needs to be real in order to have the same effects.

230

LIVE WITH PURPOSE

If food, water and shelter are vital for your physical survival, then living with purpose is essential for your psychological wellbeing.

Ask yourself what you are doing when you feel most contented or excited, or both. You'll know when you're doing something you truly love because you will be 'in the zone' and time seems to stand still. Above all, living with purpose means remembering why we are here and honouring our gifts on a daily basis. It means living in a way that's congruent with our values. That might be caring for a loved one, volunteering for a non-profit organisation or just going to work every day and fulfilling your role with passion.

231

TRAIN THE BRAIN: NUMBER TEASERS

Stretch your mind with these quick number puzzles and brain-teasers.

1: There are two swans in front of a swan, two swans behind a swan and one swan in the middle. How many swans are there?

2: You're going to the theatre and you're paying for tickets. Would it be cheaper to take one friend to the theatre twice (assuming the cost of tickets remains the same) or two friends to the theatre at the same time?

Answers: 1. Three swans. 2. Two friends at the same time, because you only have to pay for your own ticket once.

232

GET TO A GALLERY

There is more than artistic pleasure to be derived from visiting an art gallery – even a trip of 40 minutes can significantly reduce the level of stress in the body.

In one study, participants reported a 45 per cent reduction in their perceived stress levels. And the drop in cortisol levels was not only very substantial (about 32 per cent) but also very quick. Immediately following the gallery visit, stress hormone levels had fallen to below average for the time of day.

There are all kinds of galleries out there. Look up those near you and consider becoming a member to keep updated on upcoming exhibitions and receive special offers.

LOVE LAVENDER

The scent of lavender is said to have a calming effect on the senses, and is believed to be a particularly effective natural remedy for symptoms of anxiety. Tinctures or teas made using lavender are sometimes prescribed to people suffering from insomnia to help them sleep better.

Lavender can be found in plant form and as an essential oil. Lavender essential oil can be found in massage oils that help to relieve joint pain and relax aching muscles. It is also believed to act as an anti-inflammatory and can be found in skin moisturisers that help cleanse bacteria from the skin. The oil's smell is also considered an effective insect repellent – it can be applied directly to the skin to help ward off moths and mosquitoes.

Try this pretty plant's soothing effects for yourself:

- Use dried lavender leaves and flowers to make your own potpourri and enjoy the relaxing scent around your home. Adding a few drops of lavender essential oil will bring out the fragrance even more.
- Experiment with essential oil blends: peppermint and chamomile are other clean, soothing scents that combine well with lavender.
- Create a therapeutic bath experience by adding 100 grams (3.5 ounces) Epsom salts as the water is running. This magnesium-rich addition will help to relax sore and tired muscles. Then add in five drops of lavender essential oil a few minutes before you hop in to provide a beautifully relaxing scent as well as an extra skin-softening element.
- Make a lavender bag with dried lavender to slip under your pillow come bedtime. Be sure to change the lavender every few months so the fragrance remains strong.

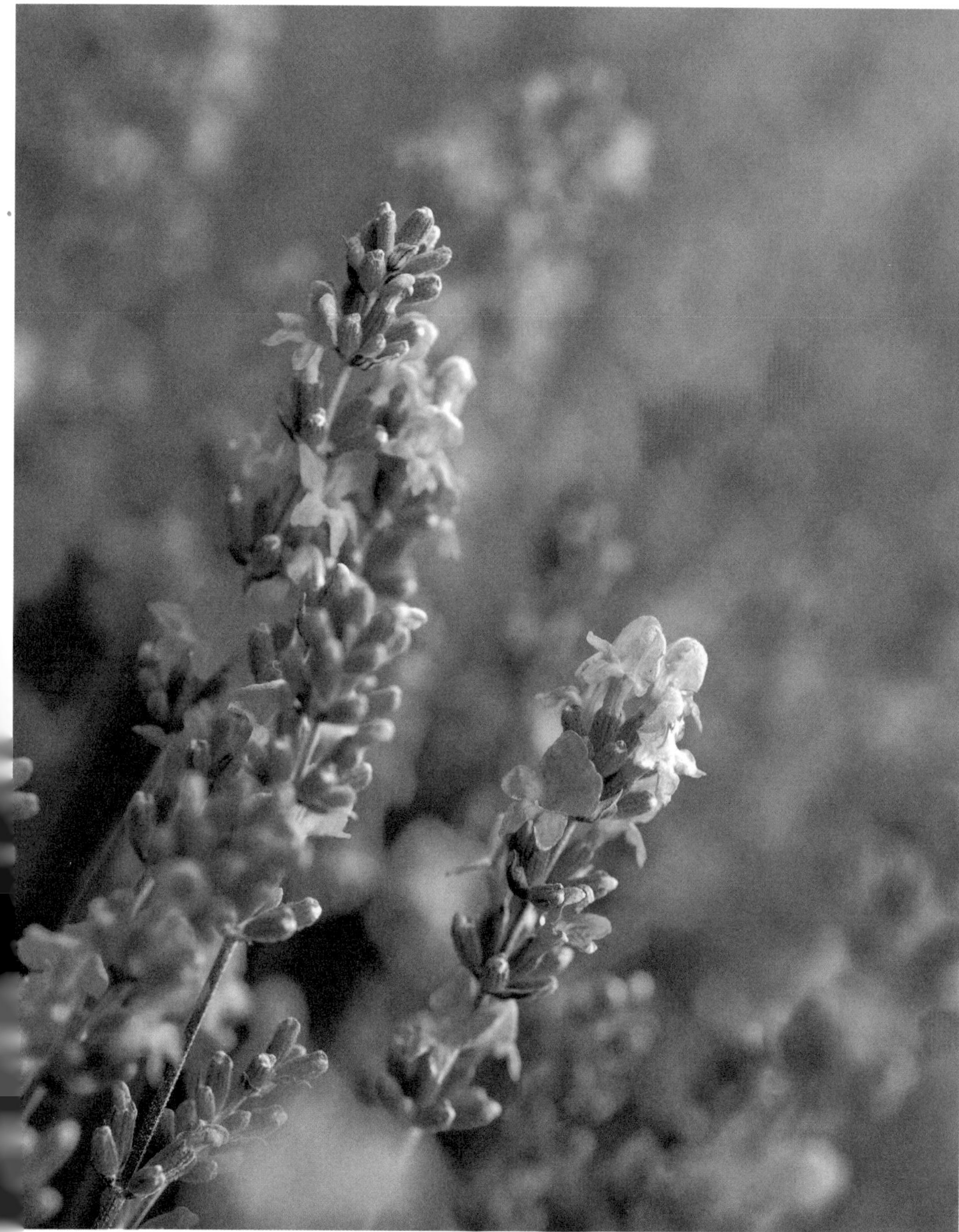

234

REVITALISE WITH A BATH

When you're tired or your muscles are aching, there's nothing quite like a long soak in a hot bath. The addition of homemade bath salts can make the experience all the more luxurious while you recharge.

Simply mix in a drop or two of your favourite essential oil(s) with a handful or two of Epsom salts and add to your running bathwater. The salts help soothe muscles and eliminate toxins from your body, while the oils add a touch of heavenly aromatherapy to nourish and stimulate your senses. Re-energise your mind and body by opting for the following:

- For an invigorating bath, choose mint or grapefruit.
- For an uplifting bath, choose geranium or ylang ylang.

235

GET THE ROYAL TREATMENT

Royal jelly is a nutritional superstar – a powerful antioxidant, it is able to restore strength and energy, improve concentration and balance the nervous system. It is produced by bees as a superfood reserved for the queen bee and newly hatched bee larvae. Royal jelly was used in ancient Chinese medicine to promote long life and protect immunity.

Nowadays, it can be found in skin creams and hair conditioners, which can be applied directly to the skin and hair. It is also used as a dietary supplement in the form of daily capsules, which can be found at most health food stores.

EXPAND YOUR VOCABULARY

An average English-speaking adult has a vocabulary of 50,000 to 60,000 words or 20,000 families of words from similar roots. But this number is tiny compared to the number of words in English in total – estimated at between 500,000 and 1,000,000, with neologisms (new words) increasing this figure by perhaps 25,000 a year. If you can get by with relatively few words, why is it worth trying to boost your vocabulary?

Studies have shown that a person's vocabulary was a very accurate predictor of general career success. Since then, a number of studies have shown correlations between people's vocabulary and their performance in exams, even in general subjects not directly related to language.

There are many enjoyable ways to increase your vocabulary. Here are a few:

- Read more books. Reading books exposes you to new words – and don't confine yourself to tried and tested authors.
- Magazines and newspapers can also boost your vocabulary. Aim to learn one new word a day or however many words you can handle.
- Crosswords and word puzzles provide new challenges.
- Whenever you come across a word you don't understand, look it up and make a note to help you remember it.
- Subscribe to free 'Word of the Day' emails from online dictionaries.

PRACTISE SELF-DISCIPLINE

Scientists have demonstrated that self-discipline can have dramatic benefits in life. For instance, people with high self-discipline are less likely to turn to drugs, alcohol and crime, and are more likely to manage their money well and get along better with other people.

If you have ever tried to give up smoking or stick to a physical exercise regime, you'll know that it takes real self-discipline. A bit like a muscle, self-discipline needs hard work, and the more you exercise it the stronger it gets. With strong self-discipline, you can control your emotions, impulses and appetites, as well as your performance.

What this means, in effect, is that by using self-discipline in practical areas of your life such as eating healthily, you can build the necessary discipline to manage how happy you feel. Self-discipline is also vital to your overall happiness, because many of the activities that boost your wellbeing (such as regular exercise) will take a while to develop into a habit.

So how do you go about increasing your self-discipline? You'll need to take small steps at the start and build up from there. The key is to set the bar high enough that you have something to aim for, but not so high that you haven't got a hope of achieving it. Here are a couple of extra tips:

- Ask your family and friends to remind you of your goal. External pressure can help you to resist old habits.
- Set yourself firm deadlines for achieving your goal.
- If you find yourself thinking about losing control, try to distract yourself by consciously thinking or doing something else.

238

LAUNCH A BLOG

Starting a blog offers you a great opportunity to express yourself and connect with people who have similar interests. It is also an effective way to keep in touch with friends and family who may be far away.

The internet offers innumerable blog platforms to suit your preferences. The majority of the most popular blogging websites are easy to set up and use. The glory of blogging is you can choose to write about anything. But whatever direction you choose to go, make sure it's something you're passionate enough about to keep up with at least a couple of times a week.

To enhance your experience, be sure to read and interact with other bloggers – in turn you can enhance your sense of community and acceptance.

239

MAKE MUSIC

Researchers now believe that musical training can be powerful when taken up at any age. It appears that learning a new instrument can enhance the brain's capacity to learn other skills. Furthermore, researchers have found that trained musicians have an increased ability to recognise nuances in musical contexts as well as detect linguistic patterns and emotional distinctions in speech. If we consider the creativity, precision and focused development of this ability, the rewards of learning such a skill can be immense. It's never too late to start!

EAT YOUR FIVE A DAY

According to the food pyramid that has been in existence in one form or another since the 1970s, your diet should include at least five portions of fruit and vegetables a day. This is to be balanced with six to 10 portions of pasta, grains and cereals; two to three portions each of protein and dairy foods and sparing quantities of fats and sugars.

In order to count towards your five a day, fruit and veg can be raw or cooked, frozen, tinned or juiced. This may not seem such a tall order, but you might fail to achieve the quota day after day.

You should try to, though, because the health benefits of fruit and vegetables are substantial. Many of them are high in fibre and low in fat; they are packed with minerals, vitamins and antioxidants. They have no artificial or added colouring or sweeteners.

In order to achieve your five a day, you should count on eating around 400 grams (14 ounces) of fruit and vegetables a day. A medium-sized fruit (apple, banana) or two small fruits (kiwi, tomato) count as one portion, while two small vegetables (new potatoes, cauliflower spears) or three heaped tablespoons of cooked vegetables (corn, peas, beans) count as one portion.

HEALTH DAY: KALE AND GINGER STIR-FRY

Kale is chock full of nutrients: its high quantities of fibre, sulphur, iron, essential vitamins and minerals make it the ideal leafy vegetable for detoxifying and protecting your body. It's also very versatile in dishes and tastes great baked as a healthy snack. Cavolo nero is a dark-leaved variety of kale.

900g (32 oz) kale, preferably cavolo nero
2.5cm (1 in) ginger root
1 tablespoon fennel seeds
6 tablespoons olive oil
½ teaspoon dried red chilli flakes
Salt and freshly ground black pepper

Wash the kale and trim away the thickest stems. Shred the leaves. Grate the ginger.

Roast the fennel seeds for one minute in a dry frying pan or wok. Then add the oil, grated ginger, chilli flakes and seasoning to the pan and cook for up to three minutes. Add the shredded kale and stir-fry for five minutes. Season to taste with salt and freshly ground black pepper.

Serves four.

242

GO WITH YOUR GUT

Studies have shown that, when meeting someone new, we make up our mind about them within milliseconds. Even after further thought, we are unlikely to revise our initial impression.

This form of unconscious decision-making kicks in for complex decisions, but some of us are prone to overthink things anyway – such as working out how we feel about someone or a situation. This can waste time and mental energy. Save on that unnecessary stress by spotting when you override your primary reactions only to reach the same conclusion much later. In similar instances, you can then rely a little more on your intuition, rather than questioning it. Sometimes, gut instinct is best.

243

TRY NEW ACTIVITIES WITH YOUR PARTNER

One of the healthiest things you can do for your relationship is to try new things together. Fresh and interesting experiences help strengthen the bond between you and your partner and create fun memories that last. Choose an activity where you are working as a pair, like scuba diving or ballroom dancing, and you'll increase these feelings of closeness through teamwork. Set new shared goals to bring you closer together and provide a sense of accomplishment.

244

DISCOVER FAMILY HISTORY

Investigating family history, like all hobbies, can help give a sense of purpose, and it is all the more rewarding in allowing you to discover your roots and understand your own past more fully.

The ever-increasing sophistication of digital information and resources available on the internet have made it much easier to search for your ancestors. To construct a family tree, begin by tracking down birth, marriage and death certificates. Documents such as parish registers, hospital records and adoption papers also provide vital clues. Plus it gives you a chance to chat about your history with family and friends, helping to maintain and strengthen relationships.

245

DAYDREAM

In a study at Harvard University, people with successful creative careers were studied to discover how much they screened out information while focusing on a task. It was found that their minds frequently wandered, and the ease with which they welcomed exterior distractions into their thoughts is believed to be indicative of flexible thinking. Similarly, a relaxed mind-set is more likely to make creative links than a completely focused one.

When you're next faced with a new task, look at it from several angles and don't get frustrated if your mind wanders – seeing where your thoughts lead and connect will keep your creative abilities active.

DAILY INSPIRATION

'Live each day as if your life had just begun.'

Johann Wolfgang von Goethe
German author (1749 – 832)

JOIN A SPORTS TEAM

It's never too late to discover your inner athlete, even if you'll never play like a pro. Joining a sports team is a fun way to break out of your mundane exercise routine and enjoy some social bonding. Many team players find that they enjoy it so much, it doesn't even feel like exercise.

Team sports develop skills that are transferable to other parts of your life, such as decision-making, communication and cooperation. Tennis, volleyball, bowling... pick one that appeals and start building new relationships and social confidence at the same time as strengthening existing skills and building fitness. You're committed to a regular schedule of exercise and to your team, so you're unlikely to lose motivation and give up.

An added bonus – you'll bond with like-minded people and always have something to talk about.

Here are some of the best team sports to keep you fit:

Basketball: Varied movements use every muscle group in the body and fast running boosts the cardiovascular system.

Rowing: A total body workout that sculpts and strengthens muscles in your arms, legs, back and core.

Football: Builds stamina, coordination, flexibility and endurance through constant motion.

Sailing: Improves non-verbal communication skills, while pulling and hoisting sails builds muscular strength and endurance.

248

RECYCLE TO HELP THE PLANET

Recycling helps the environment in many ways. For example, recycling aluminium cans not only saves energy and reduces carbon emissions but also eliminates the need to mine the bauxite ore used to create the cans. (Open-cast bauxite mining is closely linked with the destruction of the Amazon rainforest.)

Recycling aluminium uses 95 per cent less energy than producing the metal from raw materials. Glass can be recycled indefinitely since its structure does not deteriorate when reprocessed. Producing recycled paper uses 30 per cent less energy than producing new paper. So next time you are about to throw away a can, bottle or sheet of paper, take a second to sort it into the appropriate recycling bin. You will be helping to save the planet.

249

MAKE A SCRAPBOOK

Photo albums of precious moments can make you feel nostalgic – perhaps even wishing to return to those times or to be able to relive them. Some studies have shown that such feelings can brings benefits, making people feel better about themselves and their lives in general.

As well as keeping photos, why not keep other reminders of the meaningful events of your life, by pasting them into a scrapbook. Buy a blank book or album and stick in mementos you have saved from special occasions. You might also want to add in some written commentaries while the event is still fresh in your mind.

250

SWITCH OFF THE TV

Most of us are aware of the research showing that passive TV watching is bad for our bodies and for our brains. But that doesn't stop us. In fact, a Nielsen report found that the average American still watches more than 34 hours of television each week.

Television is particularly harmful for children because it steals time for activities that help develop the brain, like playing games, developing new skills and socialising with others.

Switching off the TV for a few days or weeks is a simple yet brilliant way to stimulate the mind and free up time to spend more productively. Less time in front of the box means more time to socialise, exercise, sing, play music, volunteer, read or work on those projects that have been on the backburner forever.

251

FIND AN EXERCISE BUDDY

Exercising alone is admirable, but it's easy to lose motivation – especially when it's cold or rainy outside. Get an exercise buddy and you're far more likely to stick to your fitness routine. Together, you and your buddy have twice the motivation and you won't want to let them down by not showing up for a session.

Choose your buddy through an online group, find them at work or at the gym. You could even find a few buddies and start a sports team or group. If you choose a like-minded person with strong willpower, you could triple the effects of your regular workout.

RELAX AND UNWIND: BLOWING A FEATHER BREATH

This is a gentle, cooling breathing technique that can be practised at any time you feel heavy, hot and bothered. Practising it will help to slow down your heart rate and not only cool you down but also relax both your body and mind.

- Sit in a comfortable upright position and bring one hand close to your mouth, with the thumb and index fingers together, as if holding the end of a feather.
- Purse your lips and inhale slowly through your mouth.
- Then blow out gently, making a soft 'hoo' sound, as if blowing the imaginary feather. Your fingertips should feel a cool breeze.
- Repeat until you feel calmer and cooler.

THIRSTY SKIN MOISTURISER

All skin has its own natural moisturising factor that regulates water flow from the dermis to the surface; however, as you grow older, you need to complement these natural processes by the daily application of a water-regulating moisturiser.

4 teaspoons wheatgerm oil
4 tablespoons avocado oil
25g (¼ cup) cocoa butter
1 teaspoon beeswax
2 tablespoons rose water
10 drops geranium essential oil
5 drops frankincense essential oil
5 drops sandalwood essential oil

Combine the wheatgerm and avocado oils in a heat-resistant bowl and place in a pan which has been half-filled with water. Heat, adding the cocoa butter and beeswax until the mixture is blended. Add rose water. Remove from the heat and add essential oils. Allow to cool before storing in an airtight container. Keep in the refrigerator and use within one month.

254

GET UP AN HOUR EARLIER

From world leaders to influential scientists and artists, many successful people attribute their achievements partially to waking up early. Adding just one extra hour to your waking day can have a positive impact on many aspects of your life:

- Waking up earlier gives you more time to exercise, energising both your mind and body by increasing blood circulation.
- Arriving early at work and having a quiet, peaceful hour to focus will help you plan and prepare better for the day ahead, alleviating work-related stress and increasing your productivity.
- Waking up earlier can also aid better sleep, as your body is tuned with the earth's circadian rhythms.
- Studies have shown that 'morning people' are more optimistic, proactive and better at solving problems efficiently.

255

SKIP A MEAL

Occasionally skipping a meal or fasting for a day may have a surprising effect on your health. One study showed that participants who cut their daily calorie intake by 75 per cent for two days a week showed a significant reduction in blood insulin levels. The participants not only lost weight but they also reduced their risks of diabetes and cancer that come with high blood-glucose levels and excess weight. Try skipping a meal once or twice a week and monitor how you begin to feel. However, speak to your health practitioner before undertaking any long-term fasting routine.

256

BELIEVE YOU CAN DO BETTER

Stanford University psychologist Carol Dweck has identified the existence of a much more helpful mental state called the 'growth mind-set', in which people believe that their capabilities and potential can be enhanced and developed through practice and effort. The growth mind-set allows you to try new ways of doing things if the first, second or third attempt fails.

- Recognise that it's up to you how you interpret failure. See it as a sign that you need to stretch yourself and try harder.
- Be aware that the brain, like any other muscle, gets stronger the more it is used.
- When life gets tough, remember that people are successful because they persevere.
- Learn from setbacks – pick yourself up and try again.

257

WALK THE PATH TO BETTER THINKING

Whenever you feel stressed, angry or frustrated, taking a break and going for a short walk can be one of the most effective solutions. Walking gives you enough detachment to calm down, re-evaluate and see things more clearly. Not only does it get you outside and exposed to natural light, it also boosts your energy levels, releases endorphins and primes your mind for inspiration. If at any point during the day you feel stuck or unproductive, often a change in ideas is all that's needed.

258

GROW ROSES

Growing roses can be a little like raising a family. Over time you get to know each plant – when it needs watering and pruning – and you will feel proud and excited when they bloom.

Plant roses in late autumn, before the ground has a chance of freezing, and in an area that will get at least five hours of sunshine a day. Water the plants regularly, avoiding getting water on the leaves as this can spread disease.

Lightly prune established roses in autumn; do any hard pruning in early spring when frosts have finished. Always cut just above a leaf joint, slanting down towards the plant, so that new shoots grow away from the centre, avoiding overlap. Cut away any dead wood. To keep your roses healthy, remove and destroy any leaves with blackspot, and keep aphids at bay by treating the plants with a commercial spray.

259

BRUSH UP EVERY DAY

Good dental care can help us to live longer. Our mouths are full of bacteria that may be harmful if they get into the bloodstream. Healthy gums form a barrier that the bacteria cannot cross, but if we don't look after our gums, an infection known as periodontal disease can set in, breaking down the defences. Recent research has linked periodontal infections to heart disease, diabetes and respiratory disease. Unfortunately, the risk of periodontal disease grows as we get older.

Take care of your teeth and gums by brushing often and thoroughly, flossing properly and seeing your dentist regularly.

HEALTH DAY: SHREDDED BEETROOT AND FETA SALAD

The beautiful, bright red colour of beetroots isn't just attractive to the eye, it's great for the waistline. Beets have been used over the centuries as folk remedies for anaemia, menstrual problems and kidney disorders. This root vegetable contains betacyanin, which, along with its other antioxidants, has been shown to enhance detoxing processes in the liver.

- 100g (1 cup) golden raisins
- 2 medium courgettes
- 350g (3½ cups) uncooked beetroots
- 2 medium carrots
- 1 endive lettuce
- 2 avocados
- 175g (1¾ cups) soy feta cheese, crumbled

For the dressing:

- 90ml (⅓ cup) olive oil
- 1 tablespoon Dijon mustard
- Grated rind and juice of 2 oranges
- Salt and freshly ground black pepper

Place the raisins in a bowl. Whisk together the dressing ingredients, pour over the raisins and allow to soak for 30 minutes. Cut the courgettes into strips. Grate the beetroots and carrots. Wash the endive lettuce and separate into leaves. Halve the avocados, stone, peel and cut into slices.

Mix together the salad ingredients in a large bowl. Add the crumbled cheese and add more salt and pepper if required. Drizzle the dressing over the salad and serve immediately.

Serves four.

MANAGE YOUR TIME

Being too busy can have a negative effect on your performance. Often we are not managing our time efficiently, and there are ways to reduce 'busyness' that can increase productivity and happiness in the office and at home.

- Start the day by making inroads into your big projects, leaving administrative tasks until last.
- Organise yourself – keep a notebook or a diary to jot down appointments and reminders. Take at least 30 minutes at the beginning of the day to map out your priorities.
- If you're constantly bombarded with emails and phone calls, rather than responding to everything right away, designate a specific time for answering non-urgent correspondence.
- Build buffer time into your schedule.
- Ask colleagues and friends for support and delegate effectively.
- Learn how to say 'no' to additional work.
- When setting deadlines and goals for yourself, be specific about the time of day and stick to them.
- Don't allow your calendar to fill up with meetings.
- Put blocks on social media and other distracting websites unless you use these websites for your business.

262

LOSE THE FEAR

Having ambitions is an indication of optimism, but so often we consider our dreams to be unrealistic aspirations. This suggests a reluctance to reach beyond the immediate future – being unable to see what is in front of us makes us hesitate and take smaller steps. We often overestimate the negative impact our choices will have, and decide against doing things out of fear of those potential consequences. A much-published article by a palliative care nurse examined what people regretted the most while dying, finding that many wished they'd had the courage to follow their dreams.

So today, do something bold. Don't worry if things aren't all planned out – revel in that potential, move ahead and you might surprise yourself with how well you prosper in unfamiliar waters.

263

SEND SNAIL MAIL

Throughout history, great writers have revealed their lives, thoughts and feelings through written missives. Letters can play a vital role in our modern lives, too. There's a special feeling of happiness and excitement we get when we open a personal letter. And sending a letter shows we care about the recipient because it involves more time and effort than sending an email or a tweet.

You can also write letters to people in your life as a therapeutic practice. Instead of sending the letters, discard them after writing. This is a wonderful way to express your feelings without harming anyone else's.

264

LOVE WHAT YOU DO

If there are aspects of your life or career that make you unhappy, these can be explored constructively. Self-awareness is an important part of this, as understanding yourself and your preferences allows you to work out how and what can be changed to maximise happiness. Identify which triggers improve or lower your mood, and spend more time on the activities and relationships that make you happy. Even just a week of favouring activities that you enjoy, however small they are, will accumulate to improve overall mood.

For any unpleasant tasks that can't be avoided, whether at home or work, try looking at them in a different light. You are in control of how you feel about things, so understand and harness what makes you feel good or bad about them and organise your life accordingly.

265

STRETCH: HAMSTRINGS

This exercise stretches the hamstrings, the group of muscles in the back of the legs that flex and bend the knee. You will need a long strap or belt to stretch against.

- Lie on your back on the floor with your legs straight. Bend one knee in towards your chest and hug your knee close to your body. Hold on to your lower calf and extend your leg up to the ceiling. You will feel this stretch all along the back of the leg.
- Breathe in and out and gently try to pull the leg nearer to your face. Repeat with the other leg.

266

IMPROVE YOUR SPATIAL SKILLS

Spatial thinking is what we do when we visualise shapes in our 'mind's eye' and it's a talent that's worth cultivating.

Sound spatial skills are not just for architects or engineers, they are regarded as some of the most basic reasoning abilities. Among other things, they help you to read maps, judge distances, rearrange furniture and load the dishwasher. Put simply, they make it easier to negotiate our way in the world.

Many of us haven't used these skills since we were young and played with kiddy shape-sorters. Thankfully, there is now scientific evidence to show that spatial skills are malleable and we can improve them with practice. And at the same time, we can sharpen our minds in an all-round sense and improve our competence in science and maths.

Here are some ways to improve your spatial reasoning:

- Take up a hobby like carpentry or drawing.
- Play computer games that require you to arrange shapes or objects in a three-dimensional space.
- Enrol in a class in Computer Aided Design (CAD).
- Do a jigsaw puzzle or play with a Rubik's Cube.
- Try orienteering to develop map-reading and compass-reading skills.
- Learn to read music or play an instrument.

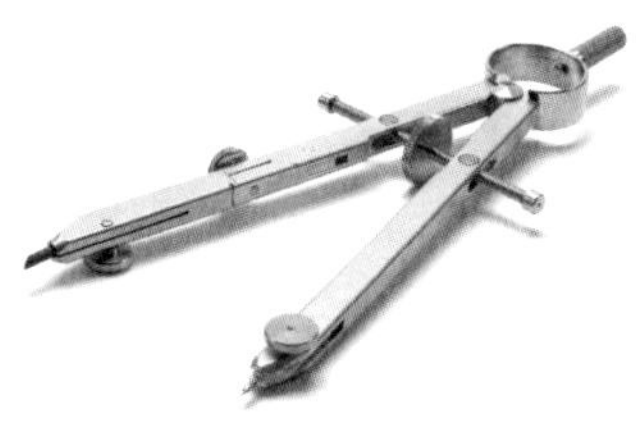

DAILY INSPIRATION

'Our doubts are traitors,
and make us lose the good
we oft might win,
by fearing to attempt.'

William Shakespeare
British playwright and poet (1564 – 1616)

268

TRAIN THE BRAIN: QUICK CONUNDRUM

Two elderly people wish to cross a river. The only way to get across the river is by boat. The boat can only take one person at a time. There is no way the boat can travel without a passenger, and there are no ropes or anything else of that nature available.

Despite all this, the two elderly people are able to cross the river. How is the possible?

Answer: They are on opposite sides of the river, so they are able to travel separately in the boat.

269

KEEP THOUGHTS FOR OTHERS

Focusing your thoughts on others can relieve stress from your own life and dramatically increase your sense of wellbeing. A study conducted in 2003 found that, out of 1,000 interviewees, those who prayed for other people had less stress and better wellbeing than those who prayed for material possessions.

Set aside a small amount of time each day to think about others and silently wish them well. One way to do this is the contemplative practice of loving-kindness or *metta*, as it is called in the Pali language – an ideal of pure love that extends out to all beings.

270

MAINTAIN A HEALTHY BANK BALANCE

Financial fitness is as important as physical health because it affects our wellbeing every day of our lives and especially our future. Like driving a car, it's a skill anyone can learn and it's never too late to start.

Having a budget means thinking about money in a logical, analytical way. Once you know exactly how much is coming in and going out, you are ready to take control and live within your means, instead of drifting along and hoping for a windfall. It also means you are able to take up exciting opportunities as they come along and are equipped for that financial rainy day.

Once you know where you're going and how you'll get there, you can direct your money to where it matters most, stay on top of bills and start putting money aside for future goals, like buying a house or going on holiday. To begin budgeting:

- Identify all income and expenses, on a monthly or annual basis.
- List your needs and the amount of money required to fulfil them.
- Be realistic and separate needs from wants.
- Design your budget to include some small pleasures so you won't feel miserable.
- Put your plan into action and stick to it.
- Review and adapt your budget from time to time, with future needs in mind.

271

PERSONALISE GIFTS

A thoughtfully chosen gift can warm the heart of both giver and recipient. Giving a gift that is beautifully wrapped makes it even more special. Your recipient instantly knows how much time, energy and effort you have put into the work and sees this as a reflection of their importance to you. It is a great boost to a person's self-worth.

The best-looking presents are ones where all of the elements complement each other in tone, texture and pattern. Once you have a colour scheme together, you can use all sorts of trimmings to finish off: strips of fabric or decorative ribbon tied around a present; a personalised tag; pretty seasonal flowers or leaves, buttons, felt shapes or sequins. The options are endless.

272

GO GREEN WITH TEA

Green tea includes antioxidant compounds called polyphenols that are believed to provide powerful protection against certain cancers and, possibly, the damage caused by LDL ('bad') cholesterol. One large-scale study in China found that people who drank green tea just once a week for six months had lower rates of rectal and pancreatic cancers than those who never drank it.

Drink up to four cups of freshly brewed green tea daily. Use one teaspoon of tea leaves per 250 millilitres (8.5 fluid ounces) of very hot water and allow to steep for 2 minutes. If you boil the water first, allow it to cool before pouring it over the leaves. Water that is hot but not boiling accentuates the delicate flavour.

JUICE DAY: MORNING GLORY

The ultimate health juice, each glass contains more than your day's requirements of vitamins A, B, C and E. It will also ward off the hunger pains too, as it is very filling; so you'll be less likely to stop for an egg and bacon sandwich on your way to work.

1 apple
1 pear
1 carrot
1 stick of celery
1 kiwi fruit
6mm (¼in) ginger root

Juice all the ingredients together. Leave in the refrigerator for 15 minutes to chill if desired, or just add ice.

For extra sweetness put the mixture in a blender and add a banana and a handful of blueberries.

Serves one as a juice and two as a blended smoothie.

Think Younger
Shrink Your Portions
Enjoy the Moment
Do It Now
Have a Glass of Red
Health Day
Enjoy Dark Chocolate
Play Computer Games
Train the Brain
Learn a Craft
Eco-friendly Bubble Bath
Value Your Friendships
Juice Day
Back Up Your Immune System
Stretch
Come Dancing
Chew Your Food Well
Find Resilience
Chill Out at the Library
Avoid Soft Drinks
Be a Philosopher
Daily Inspiration
Learn a New Language
Give a Sensual Massage
Take More Showers
Foot Exfoliator
Give a Hug
Eat Less Dairy
Clean Green
Appreciate Nature
Be Humble
Steam, Don't Fry

Play Chess
Health Day
Train Your Brain
Capture Happy Memories
Relax and Unwind
Enhance the Smell of Home
Don't Use a Calculator
Release Your Emotions
Exfoliating Body Scrub
Go Vintage
Stretch
Dine like a Pauper
Get Out of the Den
Conquer Candida
Give Gifts with Pleasure
Make a Better Life with Brains
Play Bridge
Daily Inspiration
Go to the Sauna
Have Hope
Be Bowel-Friendly
Sing Yourself Happy
Natural Face Cleanser
Print Photographs
Health Day
Join a Book Club
Learn Sign Language
Cut Out Caffeine
Lift Weights
Make Your Own Cards
Massage Your Face

Train the Brain
Daily Inspiration
Love Yourself
Open Your Chakras
Drink a Peppermint Tonic
Save on Heating
Come to the Rescue
Take a Packed Lunch
Feed Your Skin
Have a Social Media Fast
Make Bedtime a Luxury
Monitor Your Minerals
Master Sudoku
Health Day
Beware of Drugs
Find Faith
Avoid Food Additives
Love Like a Buddha
Seek Help (When You Need it)
Have a Good Sex Life
Stretch
Give Back
Daily Inspiration
Feed Your Nails
Eat Wholegrain
Feng Shui Your Home
Discover the Secrets of Ginseng
Think Critically
Live it Up!

WINTER

Winter is the season when everything just seems that much harder. It's cold outside, the days are darker and sometimes you just feel like snuggling under the covers. But staying active and looking after your health is especially important in winter, so resist the temptation to hibernate, and make sure you balance quality indoor time with outdoor activities and social events.

274

THINK YOUNGER

Thinking young doesn't mean having to squeeze yourself into the latest dance gear or saving up for cosmetic surgery. It just means keeping an open mind about life's endless possibilities.

To stay young in mind and body, you should aim to learn new skills, set new goals and relish new challenges. Embrace the latest technology, and use it to help you to achieve what you want to achieve. Scorn convention – if there is something that you really want to do, then find a way to do it. Never utter the words 'I'm too old' – sometimes it might be true, but don't dwell on it. Why talk about your age? Once you're over 18, no one needs to know it. And never use phrases like 'In my day... ' Today is your day as much as anyone else's.

275

SHRINK YOUR PORTIONS

The easiest way to stay slim is ... to eat less. Keep your meals and portion sizes small and avoid long gaps between eating. If you tend to have a large lunch and dinner, try to spread your daily intake over smaller, more frequent meals. A healthy snack in the morning and again in the afternoon will help to keep your blood-sugar level stable and you won't be ravenous when it comes to the main event. If you drink a glass of water or juice just before meals, you won't need so much food to fill you up. Think about how much you eat during an average meal and decide which elements you could cut down on without diminishing the pleasure. Notice how much food you need to feel comfortably full – and stop there.

ENJOY THE MOMENT

Do you ever feel that time is speeding up and that there are fewer hours in the day than there used to be? You might be wondering whether it's possible to slow down. Well, in a sense it is – through the process of savouring.

There is more to savouring than merely relishing the moment. It is about noticing, appreciating and enhancing positive experiences. Savouring involves intentionally slowing down and paying attention to your senses (touch, taste, sight, sound, smell). You stretch out the experience, and concentrate on noticing what gives you pleasure, whether it's sipping a glass of wine or stroking the cat. Savouring can take different forms; depending on the type of activity chosen, you can engage physically or mentally. But don't put too much effort into the process, just enjoy it for what it is.

Try the following savouring exercise to get started:

> Take a raisin. Look at it carefully. Smell it. Sense the sweet smell spreading through your nose, filling you with expectations of the taste. Put the raisin in your mouth and feel it with your tongue. Now chew carefully: notice how the taste spreads through your mouth. Observe how you feel and decide when you're ready to swallow. All of the sun's energy and the earth's nutrients collected in that little raisin are in you now.

277

DO IT NOW

Whatever it is that you've been putting off – do it now. Procrastination is renowned for making a small task balloon in size the longer we leave it, and yet we all do it – ultimately making the job grow in significance. People often think that they have to wait for the right motivation to kick in. Instead, just try starting – you'll find motivation swiftly follows as soon as you are immersed in a task.

Sometimes it's a question of adjusting your perception of the benefits and inconveniences. For many, having a to-do list proves effective, as the thought of no longer having the task to do and the sense of achievement in crossing off a completed assignment are more appealing than the exhaustion of delaying tactics. Feeling like you are proactive will encourage you to get on with other things too.

278

HAVE A GLASS OF RED

Several studies have shown that drinking one to two units of red wine a day is linked with better health and a longer life. Data from various studies consistently show a reduction of around 20 per cent in the risk of heart disease in people who drink about one unit of alcohol a day. Research suggests that the polyphenolic compounds found in red wine inhibit the development of atherosclerosis (fatty deposits that 'harden' the arteries), helping to keep the blood vessels healthy. Many of these polyphenolic compounds have an antioxidant effect, which may explain why a moderate intake of alcohol has also been linked with a lower risk of cancer.

HEALTH DAY: STUFFED CABBAGE LEAVES

Savoy cabbage is a member of the Brassica family, which is known for its high levels of antioxidants and minerals.

- 140g (¾ cup) mixed wild and basmati rice
- 1 onion, peeled and chopped
- 4 cloves garlic, peeled and crushed
- 125ml (½ cup) apple cider
- 100g (¾ cup) raisins
- 1 small head Savoy cabbage
- 600ml (2½ cups) vegetable stock

Preheat the oven to 180°C.

Put the rice into a medium-sized saucepan, cover with water and bring to the boil. Reduce the heat to a bare simmer, cover and cook for 50 minutes, topping up the water if necessary until the wild rice is tender. Drain and leave to cool. Put the apple cider into a small pan and gently fry the onion, garlic and raisins in it until the onion is soft. Stir the mixture into the rice and mix thoroughly.

Prepare a large saucepan of boiling water. Trim the stalk of the cabbage and pull off all the leaves that are large enough to stuff – there are likely to be 12 to 15. Drop the leaves into boiling water and leave for five minutes to soften. Drain, and stuff each one with a spoonful of the rice mixture. Working on a flat surface, smooth out a leaf, put the stuffing in the centre and fold up the sides – then roll up. You can trim away any thick stems that make rolling difficult. Pour a little stock into the bottom of a baking dish and arrange the cabbage rolls on top, making several layers if necessary. Pour the rest of the stock over the dish, cover with a lid or foil and bake for 30 minutes.

Serves four.

280

ENJOY DARK CHOCOLATE

The occasional dark chocolate treat can do much to lift the spirits and may even have an aphrodisiac effect. The notorious Italian lover Casanova was in no doubt about the erotic effects of drinking chocolate, describing it as 'the elixir of love'.

As well as prompting the body to make the 'feel-good' hormone serotonin, chocolate also contains phenethylamine, a chemical that, if taken in large enough quantities, would have the same psychotropic effects as drugs such as opium and LSD. Phenethylamine is quickly metabolised in the body, preventing large concentrations from reaching the brain, but it leaves us with the sense of wellbeing that many of us have associated with chocolate since childhood.

281

PLAY COMPUTER GAMES

Recent research suggests that games may actually be making children cleverer. Steven Johnson, author of the book *Everything Bad is Good for You*, points out that digital games oblige children – and adults – to manage multiple objectives at the same time. They also require players to prioritise their actions and to complete a number of tasks to win.

Some experts argue that the digital revolution has contributed to rising IQ scores around the world. Indeed, certain computer games develop exactly the type of skills that are challenged in IQ tests.

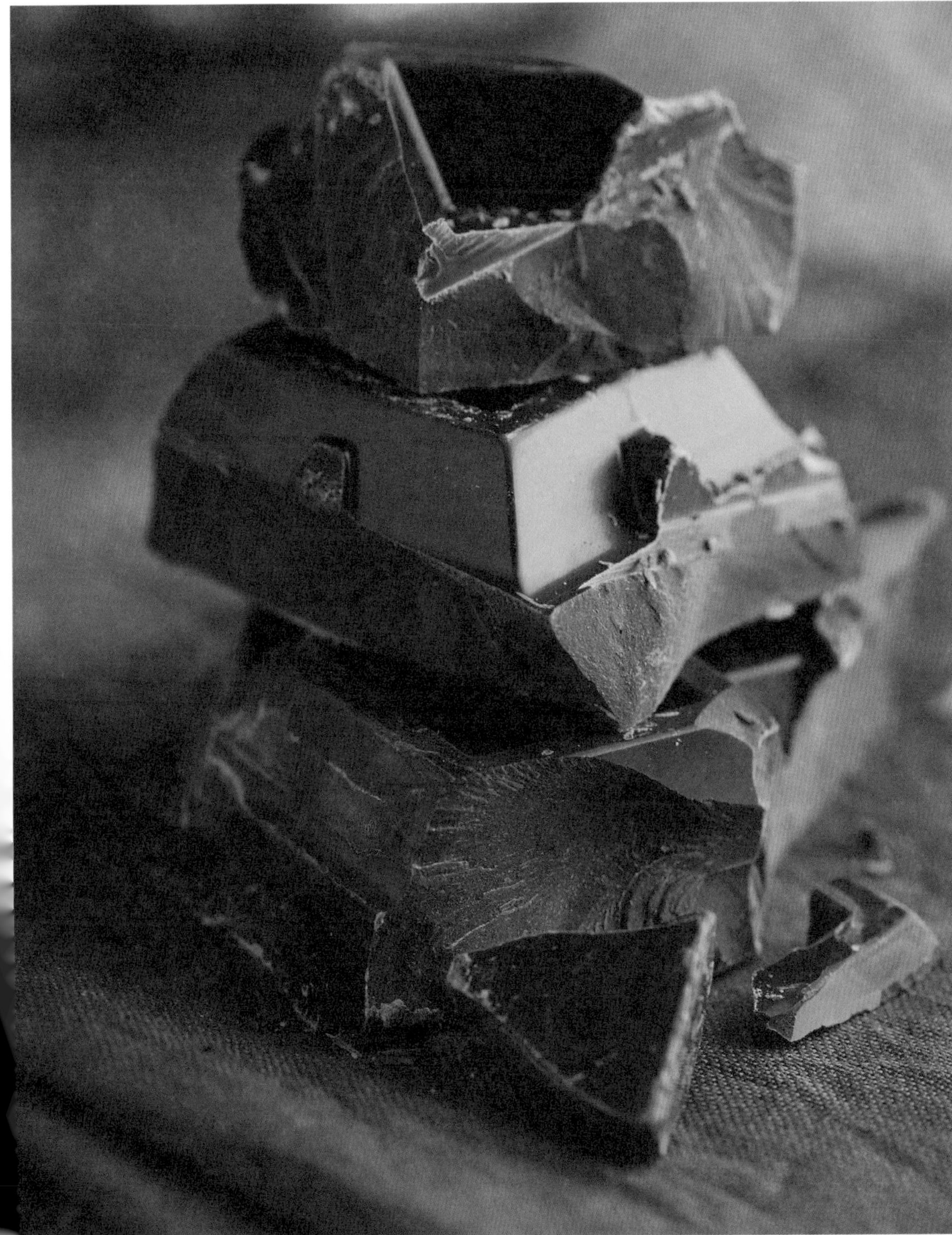

282

TRAIN THE BRAIN: HAPPY HOMONYMS

This exercise tests your ability to select the correct word from a selection of homonyms (words that sound the same but mean different things) and words that are commonly confused.

1: They ran along the road, keeping the hedge to _____ right.
(a) there (b) their (c) they're

2: Knowing who had really saved the drowning swimmer, he felt unable to _____ the award.
(a) except (b) accept (c) expect

3: 'Show me _____ you found the treasure,' said Captain Jack.
(a) where (b) wear (c) were

Answers: 1. b, 2. b, 3. a

283

LEARN A CRAFT

Craft activities can help to reduce your risk of memory loss as you grow older. Scientists from the Mayo Clinic studied 197 people between the ages of 70 and 89 who had signs of either mild cognitive impairment or memory loss. They compared them with another 1,124 people in the same age bracket who had no signs of memory problems. Researchers concluded that people who had participated in crafts or other such activities during that period of their life were 40 per cent less likely to develop memory loss than those who had not. Undertaking and persevering with projects in knitting, quilting and pottery is believed to be especially beneficial.

284

ECO-FRIENDLY BUBBLE BATH

If you worry about the list of chemicals in your favourite bubble bath and what they are doing to your skin, imagine the impact they have on the environment. Give the environment a well-deserved break by bathing in your own homemade bubble bath.

1 part Castile soap, grated

1 part distilled or filter water

Some glycerin and/or sweet almond oil

Several drops of your chosen essential oil(s)

Dissolve the grated soap in warm water then mix in the glycerin and/or oil. Add your essential oil(s). Store in a dark glass bottle for 24 hours before using. To use, shake gently and pour a generous amount under hot running water.

285

VALUE YOUR FRIENDSHIPS

Having close friends and confidants is a vital source of happiness. In one study of university students, the key difference between the happiest 10 per cent of the group and the rest was that those in the happiest group had rich and satisfying relationships with others. They also spent the least time alone and the most time socialising.

Our most valuable friends are those who bring out the best in us, who we can depend on come what may and who are kind, loving, honest and loyal. Research shows that these qualities are far more important for establishing a strong friendship than features such as the friend's accomplishments, attractiveness or status.

JUICE DAY: IRON BOOSTER

Iron is necessary for brain function: it increases the production of red blood cells, helping the delivery of oxygen to the brain. A deficiency in iron can cause weakness and fatigue. The best sources of iron are natural food sources, which often automatically contain other valuable nutrients. Vitamin C aids the body's ability to absorb iron, so fruits rich in both iron and vitamin C are particularly advantageous. Blackcurrants in particular are very high in iron, vitamin C and antioxidants. Banana, kiwi and thyme are good for boosting iron levels, with mango and orange also rich in vitamin C.

- Handful of blackcurrants
- ¼ mango
- 1 banana
- 1 kiwi fruit
- 1 orange
- ½ teaspoon fresh thyme

Put all the ingredients into a blender and blend thoroughly. Pour into a glass, and add ice if desired.

Serves one.

287

BACK UP YOUR IMMUNE SYSTEM

A well-functioning immune system is vital to good health, especially in the winter months. Our bodies are constantly assailed by invading microorganisms that can cause infections. White blood cells circulate in the blood and destroy invaders. They can 'remember' microbes that they have encountered, allowing them to deal with the same infection more quickly in future.

Regularly washing your hands can help protect you from microbes, and you can also improve the effectiveness of the immune system in the following ways:

- Eating well, giving your body a regular supply of vitamins, minerals and protein to create new cells
- Getting enough sleep
- Exercising regularly.

288

STRETCH: KNEE HUG

The knee hug stretches out the lower back, improving flexibility and releasing tight muscles.

- Lie on the floor and bend both legs up in to your chest.
- Wrap your arms around your legs, lift your head to meet your knees and breathe in.
- Breathe out and pull your knees tight in to your chest.
- Complete this stretch four times taking four deep breaths.

COME DANCING

Dancing is a fantastic way to keep physically healthy. Research shows that a vigorous dance class can burn as many calories as a gym workout, while a study of older people found that regular dancing significantly reduced levels of unhealthy fats in the blood. It also increases strength and stamina, tones leg and buttock muscles and increases lung capacity – and learning new routines helps to keep your brain sharp.

Dance and movement therapy is based on the premise that expressing yourself through bodily movement can improve your mental and emotional wellbeing. Recent studies show that hip-hop dancing has a more positive impact on wellbeing than either ice-skating or body conditioning, and that after the music has stopped, you will feel a heightened sense of contentment and a sense of accomplishment.

The social side of dancing is equally beneficial. Joining a dance class is a great way to meet new people in a relaxed and light-hearted environment. Partner-dancing in particular is especially good for communication and building relationships, whether it's through fun salsa styles or more serious ballroom dancing. As well as reducing stress, increasing your sense of balance and improving rhythm and coordination, dancing also involves music, a great mood-enhancer. Combined with the element of exercise and the social setting, the exposure to music makes dancing the ultimate feel-good activity.

290

CHEW YOUR FOOD WELL

The benefits of simply chewing a few more times are astonishing. Chewing each mouthful at least 30 times allows you to taste and appreciate your food better and makes you feel more satisfied afterwards.

Studies have shown that people who eat more slowly and chew better are generally thinner. This is because the brain has time to get the message that you are full, so you feel sated on less food.

Chewing more can also help prevent bloating and promote better digestion. When food spends longer in the mouth it has time to mix more thoroughly with saliva, which is crucial to breaking down proteins and carbohydrates and preparing food for the stomach to take on. Underprocessed food stresses the rest of the digestive tract, leaving you bloated and tired.

291

FIND RESILIENCE

What makes people respond differently to their misfortunes? Researchers believe that optimism, temperament, self-control and sense of humour all contribute to someone's ability to recover, as do positive and supportive relationships.

Happiness also enhances resilience, creating what's known as a virtuous circle. A study of the after-effects of the 9/11 tragedy in America found that resilient people generally experience more positive emotions – and that positive emotions offer protection against depression and lead to increased optimism, wellbeing and tranquillity.

292

CHILL OUT AT THE LIBRARY

If you love reading, a library can be a magical place to lose yourself, especially on a chilly winter's day. It's relaxing just to walk down the rows of books and rest in a calm environment. Choose a comfy spot, settle in and start exploring. If you have children, the library is a wonderful place to foster their love of books, and it's free.

Most libraries host regular events and activities such as book readings, community gatherings and celebrations of books where you can share your thoughts and bond with other bibliophiles.

By using a library, you are sharing books with others around you and doing your bit for recycling. Most libraries nowadays are stretched for funds, so also consider volunteering your time to help with fund-raising or donating your own used books.

293

AVOID SOFT DRINKS

Sugar is not so sweet when it comes to our health. Experts agree that sugary drinks are one of the biggest risk factors in the modern diet. Too much sugar consumption can lead to obesity, diabetes and other chronic diseases. Many of the drinks we buy and consume are loaded with sugar, including sports drinks, sodas, fruit drinks, flavoured milks and iced coffees.

There are plenty of healthy and enjoyable alternatives – try herbal teas, low-fat milk or soy milk, vegetable juice, coconut water and good old plain water. For a flavour boost, add a few drops of lemon juice, mint or fresh fruit, or sweeten your favourite drink with a little bit of honey or stevia, which are natural sweeteners.

BE A PHILOSOPHER

If your mental image of a philosopher is an old greybeard who spends his days in solitary splendour analysing abstruse arguments, think again. Around the world, young children are being taught a philosophical approach to thinking, with some remarkable effects on their intelligence.

One programme, called Philosophy for Children, was developed in the 1970s by the American psychologist Matthew Lipman. The idea is that pupils and their teacher identify a short story, a picture, a poem or an object as a stimulus for discussion. The children raise different issues about the chosen item and then select one issue for more intensive exploration. The teacher's job is to encourage the children to welcome the diversity of each others' views and to use them as the start of a process that involves questioning assumptions, developing opinions and reasoning.

All the subsequent studies about the effect of such programmes showed positive outcomes in terms of reading, reasoning, cognitive ability and self-esteem. When the researchers combined the data, they found there was a consistent effect that suggested an average gain in IQ of 6.5 points for each child.

Consider attending philosophy forums or lectures to expand your own reasoning skills. Doing so will undoubtedly enrich and expand your perspective on the world and human nature.

DAILY INSPIRATION

'Twenty years from now you will
be more disappointed by the
things that you didn't do
than by the ones you did do.
So throw off the bowlines.
Sail away from the safe harbour.
Catch the trade winds in your sails.
Explore. Dream. Discover.'

Mark Twain
American author (1835–1910)

LEARN A NEW LANGUAGE

Learning another language is obviously useful when it comes to finding the train station in a foreign land, but a wealth of research also suggests it has more fundamental benefits to your mental abilities. A study of a group of eleven- to twelve-year-old schoolchildren in the USA showed that those who learned French for 30 minutes a day for two years did better in tests that involved evaluating new information – which is considered a high-level cognitive skill – than those who did not. In another study, 18 English-speaking six-year-olds who attended a French language immersion programme had higher IQ scores than a group who attended a comparable English programme.

Experts say that learning another language can be thought of as a cognitive problem-solving activity. Many studies have shown that learning a foreign language increases critical thinking skills, creativity and mental flexibility in young children.

Researchers have also found that these benefits seem to apply to children who are bilingual. In one study of almost 100 five- to eight-year-olds, those who were bilingual in Hebrew and English had more advanced skills in processing verbal material and more discriminating perceptual distinctions than children who spoke only one language. Similarly, a Swedish study of children from Stockholm who were bilingual in Swedish and Persian found that they performed better in tests that assessed their memory.

Perhaps the benefits of learning more than one language come from the need to organise the information of two languages. It may also help in the understanding of the way language works. Bilingual children seem to develop analytical thinking about language.

Learning another language brings these benefits, so what are you waiting for? On y va! Avanti! Let's go!

297

GIVE A SENSUAL MASSAGE

One of the best ways of unwinding and getting close to your partner is to give a sensual massage. Before you start, make sure that you won't be disturbed. Then take some time to prepare the room. Create a warm, comfortable and relaxing environment with subdued lighting and soothing background music.

- Warm some massage oil between your hands and spread it evenly over your partner's body.
- Use whatever pressure feels good to your partner.
- Keep your movements steady and rhythmical, and try to keep your hands in constant contact with your partner's skin when you move to different areas of the body.
- Smooth, continuous, predictable movements are more relaxing than random strokes.

298

TAKE MORE SHOWERS

Compared with taking a bath, showering can save water and cut energy costs.

'Low-flow' showerheads, which use less water but produce a fairly strong spray, are a good alternative. They release anything from 4 to 9 litres (8.5 to 19 pints) of water per minute.

You can also save water and energy by spending less time in the shower. Cutting your shower by just one minute a day could save 77 kilograms (170 pounds) of carbon emissions a year.

299

FOOT EXFOLIATOR

Your feet carry the weight of your body around all day. Pamper them with this deliciously fresh and natural treatment.

8 large mint leaves, shredded (revitalising)
1 tablespoon brown sugar (exfoliating)
2 tablespoons oats (soothing)
2 teaspoons lemon juice (antibacterial)
2 teaspoons almond oil (moisturising)
2 tablespoons aloe vera gel (calming)

Put the brown sugar, oats and mint leaves into a bowl and mix. Add the lemon juice, almond oil and aloe vera gel and blend together until the mixture forms a thick paste. After a bath, massage the paste all over your foot. Rinse with warm water, pat feet dry and moisturise.

300

GIVE A HUG

Research has shown that physical contact can have a remarkable effect on human health and recovery. In several studies, medical patients who were touched regularly appeared to recover faster than those who weren't. Hugging alone can also lower your risk of heart disease, boost your immune system and combat stress and depression. The experience of hugging generates feel-good hormones like endorphins and oxytocin, which produce feelings of happiness and bonding. Hugging also lowers stress hormones like cortisol, which are known to increase blood pressure. So what's an effective stress-buster after a long day's work?
A good, long hug.

301

EAT LESS DAIRY

We have always thought that dairy is a necessary part of our diet and it has been particularly lauded for its calcium content and supposed role in strengthening bones. It is a prominent feature in Western diets, but new research reveals that consuming too much is not good for you. For example, it has, converse to our beliefs, been associated with osteoporosis. If you eat too much, your kidneys cannot neutralise all the acid that dairy produces. Consequently calcium is drawn from the bones to neutralise your body's pH, to the detriment of the bones.

Dairy is also responsible for many of our modern-day allergies and has been linked to eczema, asthma and various bowel issues. Those with dairy intolerance should substitute milk with fresh goat's milk and cheese. In general, it's best to favour unpasteurised, hormone-free, full-fat milk.

302

CLEAN GREEN

Switching your cleaning products to natural, non-toxic alternatives can have big benefits for your health and the environment. The harmful effects of mainstream cleaning products are now well known and there are plenty of effective 'green' products on sale.

Only buy non-toxic, biodegradable products and avoid those containing petroleum or petroleum by-products. It's easy to make your own all-purpose cleaner by mixing vinegar and bicarbonate of soda in warm water. Use plants to filter indoor air, and make your home cleaner and greener. Finally, remember to dispose of your old toxic cleaning products responsibly.

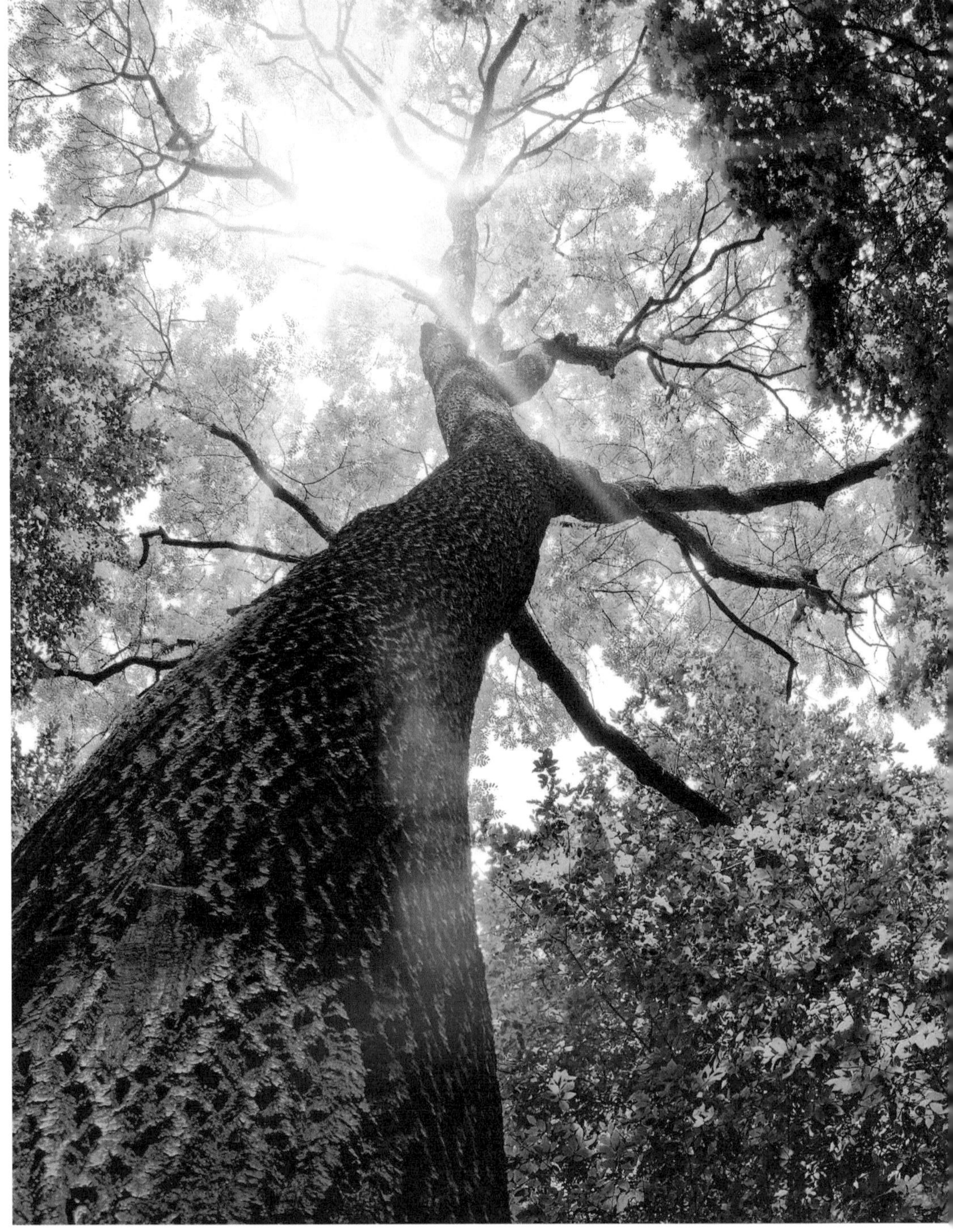

303

APPRECIATE NATURE

'I think that I shall never see a poem lovely as a tree,' wrote the American poet Alfred Joyce Kilmer in February 1913, while overlooking a wooded hillside. Kilmer was saying something more profound than he may have realised. It transpires that gazing at nature has a remarkable capacity to restore concentration.

Neuroscientists say that the human brain has two levels of attention: directed attention, which we use to focus on work, and involuntary attention, which happens when we respond instinctively to, for example, natural beauty. Directed attention is a resource that needs nurturing. According to 'attention restoration theory', appreciation of the countryside helps to renew this resource by capturing our involuntary attention and giving our directed attention a temporary respite.

304

BE HUMBLE

Studies have shown that success and humility are not mutually exclusive. What's more, humility is believed to lead to greater happiness and wellbeing by generating a number of improvements to an individual's quality of life, such as increased optimism, improved friendships and intimate relationships, greater satisfaction and morale at work, greater empathy, compassion and altruism and decreased anxiety, fear, depression and instances of conflict.

305

STEAM, DON'T FRY

Steaming food is one of the healthiest ways of cooking and has been used in Chinese and African cuisines for centuries. It's also one of the simplest cooking methods, requiring only a pan, some water and a heat source. Skilled cooks know that steaming is not just for vegetables – you can cook almost anything this way, from meat and seafood to grains and legumes.

Foods that are steamed are much healthier than foods that are fried or roasted because there's no oil involved. Lowering your fat intake can help you to lose weight and lower cholesterol. Not only that, steaming also helps the foods retain vitamins and minerals better than other cooking methods.

Winter is the ideal time to experiment a little. You can add extra taste to steamed food by adding spices to the water you use.

306

PLAY CHESS

People have been playing chess for over a thousand years. New research indicates that playing chess can actually make you smarter. In school-based studies around the world, researchers found that it can help improve reading, mathematical ability and other aspects of thinking. Some chess masters also argue that playing the game helps develop general intelligence, self-control, analytical skills and concentration.

HEALTH DAY: VEGAN POTATO SALAD

Potatoes often get a bad reputation for being fattening, starchy and worthless, but in reality potatoes are fat-free and packed full of nutrients, such as potassium, vitamin C and vitamin B6.

- 4 large new potatoes
- 3 red-skinned apples
- 1 lemon
- 2 sticks of celery, trimmed and sliced
- 55g (2 oz) hazelnuts or pecans, roughly chopped

For the vegan mayonnaise:

- 90 ml (3.2 fl oz) chilled soya milk
- 1 clove garlic
- ½ teaspoon mustard
- 2 tablespoons lemon juice
- 160ml (5.6 fl oz) vegetable oil

Boil the potatoes with the skins on. Leave to cool and then slice. Core the apples and slice thinly, again leaving the skins on. Cut the lemon in half and squeeze one half over the apples to stop them discolouring.

To make the mayonnaise, put the chilled soya milk, garlic and mustard into a blender with the rest of the lemon juice. Blend briefly. Then, keeping the motor running, slowly drizzle in the oil and continue blending until the mixture thickens.

Toss all the salad ingredients together with three tablespoons of vegan mayonnaise and serve immediately.

Serves four.

308

TRAIN YOUR BRAIN: MENTAL ACUITY

How sharp are your mental faculties? Solving these puzzles should help you to make an assessment.

1: You have eight books. How many ways can you arrange them from left to right on a shelf?

2: Some bacteria in a bowl divide themselves every minute into two equal parts that are the same size as the original bacteria, and which also divide the next minute and so on. The bowl in which this is occurring is full at 12 p.m. When was it half full?

Answers: 1 There are 40,320 ways to arrange the books. 2 It was half full one minute earlier

309

CAPTURE HAPPY MEMORIES

Keeping a diary can act as a positive force in your life. By taking time to appreciate happy experiences, you may increase the positive emotion associated with an occasion. Studies have also shown that it can have long-term physical benefits, including reduced fatigue and tension, improved work performance and improved health for people with asthma or rheumatoid arthritis.

Keeping a diary, even if it's for your eyes only, can help you to find the insights to overcome any painful emotions associated with an experience. Be careful to write about upsetting experiences in a free-form way, however. Otherwise, you might get stuck in a trough of dwelling on what went wrong.

RELAX AND UNWIND: SUN BREATHING

Sun breathing is a stimulating breath that helps to increase energy and vitality by warming the body, alleviating feelings of anxiety and making the mind more alert.

- Sit in a comfortable, upright position. Close your eyes if it feels right and breathe naturally.
- Rest your right hand on your right knee, keeping your hand relaxed and open, whether face up or down.
- Raise your left hand and place your thumb gently against your left nostril. Breathe in slowly, taking a full breath through your right nostril.
- Gently close your right nostril with the ring finger of your left hand. Hold for a second, then slowly release the ring finger and breathe out through your right nostril until your lungs are empty.
- This is one round of breathing. As a beginner, practise 10 rounds. As the breathing technique becomes more comfortable, increase the duration to between three and five minutes.

ENHANCE THE SMELL OF HOME

Replace factory-made air fresheners with homemade potpourri. You will be doing the environment a favour by sending fewer plastics to the landfill site. If you select your essential oils wisely, you can enjoy combining a range of different scents to match the changing seasons and imbue the atmosphere of your home with a relaxing sense of calm and security.

First, select your ingredients (some can be bought pre-dried but you may wish to pick and dry others yourself), and then mix together in a large bowl until you're happy with both the look and scent. Have fun experimenting with this.

Transfer the mix to a sealable jar, close the lid and leave in a cool, dark place for several weeks to let the scents infuse and intensify. Stir every few days and check the aroma's progress – if the scent isn't strong enough for your liking, add a drop more of your chosen oil(s) and leave for longer. Try these combinations:

- Warm and spicy for a soothing aroma: dried, chopped orris root; dried orange slices; whole cloves; cinnamon sticks; sweet orange or ylang ylang oil
- Light and zesty for an energising aroma: dried, chopped orris root or dried lavender; dried lemon slices; dried rose petals; dried geranium leaves; lemon or lavender oil.

312

DON'T USE A CALCULATOR

Do you reach for the calculator or smartphone when doing arithmetic? Scientists agree it's best to err on the safe side by using your brain and calculating sums in your head. Research has shown that doing arithmetic this way is good for mental agility and helps develop the right brain, boost memory levels and sharpen concentration.

Some maths teachers hold opposing views on calculators. One side argues that calculators are simply useful, time-saving tools for students. The other side suggests that calculators strip students of curiosity about how maths works because they don't have to work to find the answer. The debate rages on, but assuming you don't teach maths, it's worth making the effort next time you're adding up the bill or working out the budget.

313

RELEASE YOUR EMOTIONS

Increasingly, the act of crying while angry, sad or stressed is being recognised as beneficial, as it provides both physical and emotional catharsis and occupies an integral role in the healing process. A study by Dr Frey of Minnesota University found that emotional tears differ from reflex tears (those stimulated by irritants such as chopping onions): chemicals linked to stress are actually removed from the body through emotional tears, explaining why people usually feel better after crying. As well as releasing pent-up emotion, crying is a way of re-establishing calm, improving mood and relieving suffering – while lowering stress-related symptoms like heightened blood pressure and pulse rate. So don't bottle it up!

314

EXFOLIATING BODY SCRUB

Natural ingredients such as nuts and oatmeal can be used to exfoliate your skin without irritating it. The oil in the nuts will also provide a moisturising film so that your skin will not dry out.

- 100g (1¼ cup) finely ground nuts (try almonds)
- 50g (½ cup) oatmeal
- 50g (½ cup) wholemeal flour

Blend the ingredients until they are reduced to a coarse mixture. Pour into a glass jar with a screw top. The mixture can be stored in a fridge or freezer.

To use, scoop out a handful of the mixture and put it in a bowl, adding water to make a paste. Rub it over your body to loosen any dry or flaking skin. Wash off in the shower or bath.

315

GO VINTAGE

In a world that focuses on conspicuous consumption, wearing vintage is one way of acting consciously and responsibly. Choosing pre-loved clothing from a charity shop means you are recycling and reducing the consumption of natural resources used to produce new clothing. Knowing that you have saved those items from going to landfill is incredibly satisfying. To complete the cycle, when you no longer wear a garment, you can donate it back to a charity shop!

When you consider that you're saving money and donating to a good cause too, going vintage makes good (fashion) sense.

316

STRETCH: SPINAL TWIST

Twisting poses energise the body, increase the range of motion and flexibility in the spine, relieve stiffness in the neck and shoulders, improve the nervous system and aid digestion.

- Start seated with your legs straight in front of you and your feet hip-width apart, then bring your left leg over your right leg and tuck your right leg in. Keep your spine erect but do not lift your shoulders. Press down into the left hand, left foot and right heel to lift and lengthen the spine. Exhale as you revolve the spine to the left. Keep the shoulder blades close to the spine.
- Twist only as far as you comfortably can. Take extra care if you have abdominal or back problems. Return to your starting pose and repeat the spinal twist on the other side.

317

DINE LIKE A PAUPER

There's a popular saying that one should eat like a king for breakfast, a prince for lunch and a pauper for dinner. The idea behind this is that calories in foods eaten earlier in the day are processed more efficiently than foods eaten at night.

There are studies to back up this old adage, with health benefits such as increased energy, better digestive health and weight loss.

Eating a smaller dinner can also improve sleep quality and ensure you have an appetite for breakfast, the most important meal of the day. Also, don't eat anything after 8 p.m. when your digestive system has slowed down in readiness for sleep as it can disturb your digestive cycle and make it more difficult to fall asleep.

318

GET OUT OF THE DEN

Just because it's cold outside doesn't mean you have to hibernate and watch TV. Take advantage of the season to enjoy winter sports and activities, including some outdoor fun.

Snow sports are exciting and invigorating, so try skiing, tobogganing or snowboarding. Build a snowman, catch snowflakes on your tongue or collect pine cones. You don't have to go to an expensive resort, you can have fun anywhere there's snow. And when you're done, nothing beats the feeling of coming in from the cold and sipping a hot drink as you relax by the fire.

Indoor activities are the obvious solution to winter weather and they can be as energetic as you like – from a full workout at the gym to watching a film.

- Join a sports team and play indoor football, netball or basketball.
- Go bowling or skating.
- Attend a free cultural event or visit a museum.
- Watch a film that's amusing or uplifting.
- Register for a workshop and learn a new craft.
- Join a choir and sing to lift your spirits.
- Cook a warming soup or bake a healthy treat.
- Do your Christmas shopping online wearing your pyjamas.

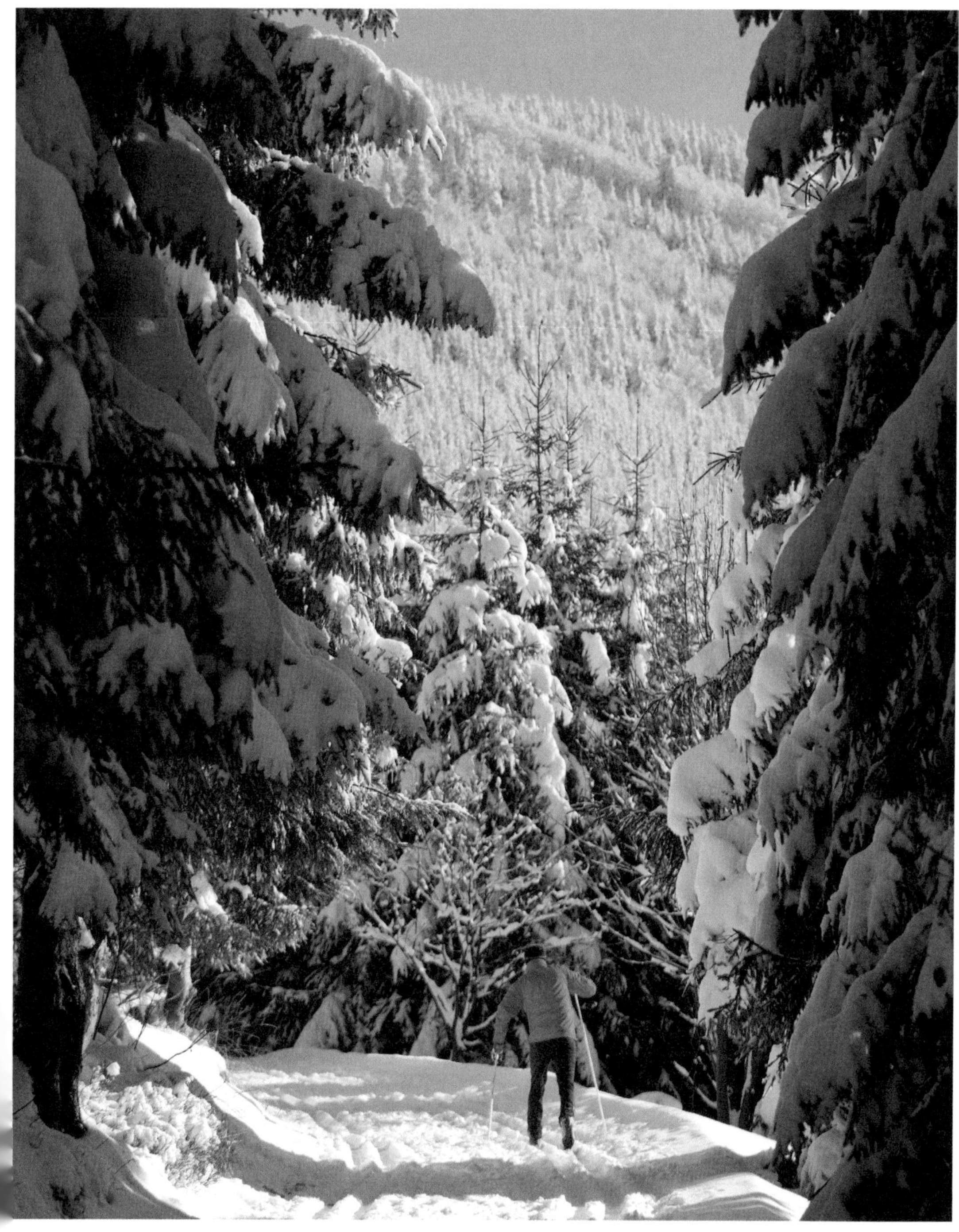

319

CONQUER CANDIDA

Candida, a type of fungus, lives in most humans and, in moderate numbers, helps with digestion. However, an overgrowth can cause a whole host of health problems, including yeast infections, bloating, severe allergic reactions and even depression. Candida overgrowth occurs when 'friendly' bacteria in your body cannot keep the candida population under control. This can be caused by a number of factors: you may have taken antibiotics that killed off too many healthy bacteria or you may consume a diet high in sugars, carbs and alcohol, all of which either harm healthy bacteria or feed candida. If you know or suspect you have a candida overgrowth, you can begin to make choices that allow the gut's friendly bacteria to grow back: cut out sugar and alcohol, reduce your carb intake, take probiotic supplements to restore your healthy bacteria and/or speak to your doctor about anti-fungal medication.

320

GIVE GIFTS WITH PLEASURE

There is an old saying that it's better to give than to receive. Best of all is the pleasure to be had from giving something that you've made yourself. Not only can you save money by making your own gifts but also you can take satisfaction from the knowledge that they were created with love and care for particular recipients. These are easy to make at home and doubly rewarding as gifts:

- Food items like jams, preserves, cupcakes or biscuits
- Cushion covers or potpourri sachets
- Culinary herbs grown from seed
- Themed photo albums or photo collages

321

MAKE A BETTER LIFE WITH BRAINS

Why should it be that clever people live longer? One explanation is that they know what to do to keep healthy, access precious resources, including healthcare, and fight for the best treatment.

Wealth has something to do with it – people with higher IQs tend to get better-paid jobs and can afford a healthier lifestyle and better medical treatment than those born into poverty or difficult social circumstances. But researchers at the London School of Economics (LSE) found that an above-average IQ is in itself important in dealing with the hazards of modern life. In developed countries, IQ was seven to eight times more strongly related to life expectancy than income was. So break out your books and keep on expanding your brain – it could mean a longer life.

322

PLAY BRIDGE

Playing bridge regularly helps to keep your memory active and your brain alert. The American business magnate Warren Buffett believes that it is an invaluable training for teamwork and analytical thinking. Also, a study by the University of California at Berkeley showed that playing bridge can even boost the immune system. Twelve women in their seventies and eighties were asked to play bridge for an hour and a half. Afterwards, two-thirds of the participants had increased levels of T-cells in their blood – the cells used to fight infection. So get a group together and play a game of bridge – it may extend both the quantity and quality of your life.

DAILY INSPIRATION

'We can't become what we need to be by remaining who we are.'

Oprah Winfrey
American talk show host, producer, media proprietor (1954–)

GO TO THE SAUNA

Although they have been around for years saunas have recently come into their own, with many people realising their health benefits. Resting in a heated environment helps to relax tired muscles. It also eliminates toxins. The heat increases your circulation, moving blood and oxygen around your body, ultimately increasing the removal of toxins through bodily waste and the skin. With your blood circulation increased by around 75 per cent, of which 70 per cent reaches the skin, toxins simply find it easier to leave the body through your pores. As your body heats up, your pores open, and water and toxins escape. Because you lose around 30 millilitres (1 fluid ounce) of water during a 10-minute sauna session, it is important to drink filtered water while you're in the room and afterwards.

Short bursts of heat are better than long periods in a sauna, mainly because you'll reduce your chances of becoming dehydrated and drying your skin out. As the air inside is very arid (around 80°Celsius/170°Fahrenheit), there is a danger of releasing too many toxins from your system. Ideally, stay in for no longer than 20 minutes. If 20 minutes in one sitting seems interminable, break it up into five-minute chunks, and plunge into a cold pool or shower to 'shock' your system. Your skin will be glowing and your mind will be extremely awake!

- Take a bottle of water to sip during your visit.
- Don't eat a heavy meal or drink alcohol before entering a sauna.
- If you feel faint, light-headed or nauseous at any time, leave the sauna immediately.
- Avoid saunas if you're pregnant, have heart problems, diabetes, epilepsy, respiratory problems or skin problems such as eczema.

HAVE HOPE

Being hopeful benefits your psychological wellbeing by helping to banish self-criticism and negative emotions, leading to a higher sense of achievement and lower incidences of depression. Being hopeful also benefits your physical health. According to research, hopeful people cope with stress better, reducing the harmful effects that stress has on the body – these vary from chronic pain and headaches to inflammation of the circulatory system. Hopeful people also, generally, enjoy longer life spans and fewer incidences of cardiovascular disease.

So, if things aren't going as you'd wish, don't give up hope – doing so may have a profound impact on your mental wellbeing and physical health. Here are some tips for finding hope when a situation is looking difficult to achieve:

- Devise an overall plan to resolve the situation and decide what you want to achieve by it.
- Divide your goal into smaller, more manageable chunks so that, as you achieve each small goal, you will become more hopeful that you can achieve your overall one.
- Tell your family and friends about your goal – they can provide moral support if your hope starts to dwindle.
- Have a strategy in mind for when things go wrong, so that you can take instant action; frame any obstacles you meet as challenges to be overcome.
- Remember to take it easy on yourself.

326

BE BOWEL-FRIENDLY

Included in the top three on the list of common cancers, bowel cancer still proves fatal in about 50 per cent of cases, despite modern treatments and, as in all such cases, early diagnosis may mean the difference between life and death.

Think first about the bowel-friendly changes to your lifestyle. Aim for a diet with less red and processed meat and a lot more vegetables and fibre. Regular physical activity and weight control are also important for bowel health. As well be alert to signs of trouble, especially if you have a family history of bowel cancer. Research shows that sending off a faecal sample for testing for occult blood every two years can reduce your risk of dying from bowel cancer by 15 per cent. If you develop symptoms such as a change in a regular bowel habit or passing blood or mucus when defecating, seek advice from your doctor.

327

SING YOURSELF HAPPY

Singing is not only fun, it has also been proven to relieve stress and enhance wellbeing. Research shows it can have some of the same effects as exercise, such as the release of mood-boosting endorphins. It is also an aerobic activity and increases oxygen levels in the blood.

Deep breathing is essential to sing properly and this can also reduce anxiety and bring about relaxation. Singing therapy has been successfully used to overcome depression and anxiety, and even treat clinically serious mental-health problems – so sing it loud, and sing it proud!

328

NATURAL FACE CLEANSER

The high acid content in this recipe – lactic acid in the milk combined with fruit acid in the tomato – gives the lotion a gentle cleaning action. Test on the inside of your arm for any allergic reaction before using it on your face. It is recommended for normal and oily skins.

1 medium very ripe tomato

150ml (5 fl oz) fresh whole milk

Juice or blend the tomato. Strain through a piece of muslin or tea towel and discard the pulp. Add the tomato juice to an equal amount of milk. Store in a covered container in the fridge for up to five days.

Apply to the face and neck with cotton-wool pads once or twice a day. Leave on for 10 minutes, then rinse off with water and pat dry.

329

PRINT PHOTOGRAPHS

The increasing sophistication of digital cameras and mobile phones allows us to take hundreds of photographs in a day. This, coupled with computer programs that let us manipulate images and post them freely on social media networks, threatens the survival of the traditional photo album.

Creating a physical (as opposed to digital) album by selecting, arranging and labelling favourite photographic prints can be a delight. It will give you and your loved ones pleasure to look back on and will prompt memories that you can share together.

330

HEALTH DAY: ASIAN STEAMED CARROTS

Not just for rabbits, carrots should feature regularly in your diet, too. These root vegetables are naturally high in fibre and minerals, but they also contain high levels of the antioxidant beta-carotene, which metabolises as vitamin A in your body, and is important for growth, your immune system and good vision. It is the beta-carotene that gives a carrot its colour – the richer and darker the colour of the carrot, the higher the level of beta-carotene. One carrot alone fulfils your body's daily vitamin A needs. Your body absorbs more beta-carotene when you eat carrots cooked rather than raw, so it is best to steam or boil them. A small amount of fat will aid absorption.

450g (1lb) whole baby carrots
2 cloves garlic
2.5cm (1in) cube root ginger
small bunch of coriander
1 tablespoon butter
juice and zest of one lime
salt and black pepper

Steam the carrots whole for 10 minutes, or until tender. Finely chop the garlic, ginger and coriander and cook in butter for a minute or so. Stir in the lime zest and juice, season to taste and pour the mix over the cooked carrots.

331

JOIN A BOOK CLUB

It's now recognised that stories can communicate and engage more powerfully than facts or figures, and reading fiction is an efficient way not to simply escape real life but to help understand it. Fiction offers a whole host of lives to experience, and it is through understanding other people that we develop greater empathy and emotional intelligence.

Book clubs are a great way to meet people, consider what you read and read things you wouldn't normally. Even just with a friend, discussing a book or film together will formulate your ideas and improve communication. Talk through what and how a book has made you feel, and why characters have acted as they did. It will also keep you open to new ideas – not just understanding a situation from your angle but also learning to regard it from different perspectives.

332

LEARN SIGN LANGUAGE

Sign language is an essential tool for communicating with the hearing impaired, who are often marginalised. However, you don't have to be a professional interpreter to experience the benefits of learning it. Like any form of bilingualism, the act of signing can enrich and enhance cognitive processes, creative thinking and problem-solving abilities. It's also a wonderful way to discover another culture and gain new insights into the lives of others. Learn it for your own pleasure, to increase your skillset or simply for the beauty of the language.

333

CUT OUT CAFFEINE

Caffeine is present in coffee, teas and energy drinks, all of which are consumed regularly by a large proportion of the population. As a stimulant, caffeine makes you feel alert in the short term, but it also increases heart rate and blood pressure. Gradually kicking your caffeine habit will improve your ability to focus without it, and there are plenty of natural ways to keep your body energised:

- Make sure you are eating enough foods that contain vitamin B12, which is found in meat, fish, eggs and dairy products.
- Herbal teas containing ginkgo biloba or ginseng are naturally invigorating.
- Start your mornings with a stretch. Stretching stimulates oxygen metabolism in the blood. This prompts wakefulness and prepares your body for the day.

334

LIFT WEIGHTS

Lifting weights is also known as resistance training. It is based on the principle that muscles in the body will work to overcome a resistant force when they are required to do so. By practising resistance training repeatedly and consistently, your muscles naturally become stronger.

Research shows that lifting weights can also improve bone density and joint mobility, which is especially important as you age. Women in particular can benefit from this type of strengthening, gaining lean muscle mass and helping to maintain flexibility and balance. In addition to all of these physical health benefits, you will also enjoy a fitter, leaner appearance.

MAKE YOUR OWN CARDS

The time you spend on a creative activity, the attention to detail, the desire to get it just right – all of these things have a value that is borne out in the finished product and can be very rewarding. The undertaking can also be very therapeutic. You can lose yourself in the work that you are doing; your mind is focused yet allows you to move subconsciously from one step to the next. One of the easiest crafts to take up is card making. The materials are not expensive and there are no particular skills to master before you set out. You will need:

- Good-quality card
- Scissors
- Glue
- Coloured pens
- Attractive alphabet stickers or interesting letters cut from old newspapers and magazines
- A few nice old buttons, scraps of fabric and pieces of ribbon

Cut a piece of card to the desired size and fold it neatly.

Decide on a message for the front of the card, writing it in coloured ink or spelling it using cut-out letters or stickers. It pays to plan this in pencil first.

Embellish the card with fabric, buttons, ribbon or other twinkly bits and pieces that you have to hand. Let your imagination run wild, taking inspiration from the recipient's personal preferences.

Sign and date the back of the card as well as writing your special greeting inside.

336

MASSAGE YOUR FACE

If you suffer from insomnia or anxiety or are simply feeling tired, give yourself a facial massage with a nourishing mixture of two drops rose essential oil and two drops neroli essential oil added to 10 millilitres (1 dessertspoon) of a base oil such as jojoba. It will stimulate circulation and create a healthy glow.

Using the fingertips of both hands, apply the oil to your face with gentle pressure, keeping the oil away from the eyes.

Start in the centre of the forehead and move out to the temples. From the nose, move out to the cheeks. From the chin, move up the jawline to the ears.

Repeat each movement three times.

Massage the same three areas of the face in turn with circular strokes.

337

TRAIN THE BRAIN: QUICK CONUNDRUM

Rachel drives 113 miles from Pittsburgh to Cleveland averaging 30 miles per hour.

How fast must she drive on the return trip to average 60 miles per hour overall?

Answer: It's impossible for Rachel to average 60 miles per hour overall. She can only double her average speed for the whole journey if she does the return leg in no time at all.

DAILY INSPIRATION

'Physical fitness is not only one of the most important keys to a healthy body, it is the basis of dynamic and creative intellectual activity.'

John Fitzgerald Kennedy
American president (1917–1963)

LOVE YOURSELF

As we go through life trying to tackle all its obstacles and challenges, facing our successes and failures, we often tend to forget just how wonderful we are. We focus on our weaknesses, rather than boosting our energy by knowing our strengths. However, studies suggest that positive thoughts are important for maintaining self-esteem, as well as making it easier for us to bond with each other. They may also make us more creative and productive, and increase our motivation and persistence. Try taking these small steps on your journey to loving yourself:

Focus on the positive: Write a list of everything that is good about you and look at it whenever you feel insecure.

Meditate each morning and evening: In the morning, take time to reflect on what is good about your life, what is good about you, why you are fortunate. In the evening, clear your thoughts, let your mind be at peace.

Embrace change and be flexible: It leads to progress. It gives you fresh perspective. Don't close yourself off and get set in your ways. The world changes. People change. Your life will and should change. Enjoy new adventures and challenges.

Expand your interests: Painting, piano or photography: it doesn't matter what you choose, just be brave and start something new. If you do not enjoy it, stop and move on to something else. If you do, let yourself flourish. This positive reinforcement will boost your self-esteem, having a positive effect all other areas of your life.

340

OPEN YOUR CHAKRAS

According to Hindu belief, Chakras are energy points in the body that regulate the flow of energy. It is believed that blocked energy causes illness, but you can open chakras and restore their holistic interdependence through awareness and understanding. Each chakra governs an organ, gland or system in the physical body, and is associated with a colour. Implementing relevant colours around the home, in food and in visualisation is believed to encourage balance. Strength and control is achieved through harmony of the main energy centres. Here are examples of some:

'Solar Plexus': Pancreas – Yellow – Digestion, Self-Confidence

'Heart': Chest – Green – Circulation, Complex Emotions

'Throat': Thyroid – Blue – Growth, Communication

'Crown': Top of head – White or Violet – Consciousness

341

DRINK A PEPPERMINT TONIC

Peppermint tea offers an effective relief from indigestion, nausea and other digestive complaints. It is also used as a decongestant by people suffering from colds and flu. You can drink up to four cups of tea a day after meals. The major active ingredient of peppermint is its volatile oil, largely made up of menthol, which stimulates the flow of natural digestive juices and bile. Peppermint tea can be made by steeping one or two teaspoons of dried peppermint leaves in 250 millilitres (8.5 fluid ounces) of very hot water for at least two minutes before drinking – but make sure you cover the cup to stop the volatile oil from escaping.

342

SAVE ON HEATING

Turning down your central-heating thermostat by just three degrees – and adding more layers of clothing if you feel chilly – is the single most effective way to save money on domestic bills while reducing your carbon footprint.

Heating accounts for around two-thirds of energy bills in many homes, especially in colder climates, and domestic heating systems emit billions of tonnes of carbon dioxide into the atmosphere each year.

According to the Energy Saving Trust, the UK's domestic energy watchdog, installing a room thermostat (if you don't already have one) is one of the most effective ways to cut heating costs. In most homes, you can save about two per cent of your heating bills for each degree that you lower the thermostat for at least eight hours each day.

343

COME TO THE RESCUE

Knowledge of first aid may one day make the difference between an individual's life and death. And, since by far the majority of accidents happen in the home, that individual may well be someone you know. First aid does not require a great deal of training – much of it is common sense – but it is worth learning a few basics. The British Red Cross and St John Ambulance organise hundreds of courses throughout the UK – for the general public, for first aiders in the workplace and for young people – the simplest of which is a brief session covering everyday first aid. Courses can be booked online and some of them are available on the societies' websites or as mobile-phone apps.

TAKE A PACKED LUNCH

Making your own lunch and taking it to work has so many benefits. To begin with, it's usually healthier than buying a ready-made lunch (and you know what's in it). Secondly, it's far cheaper and can save you a lot of money over the year. And thirdly, it is better for the environment because it reduces packaging waste, which contributes to landfills and pollutes our oceans and waterways.

Make a commitment to set aside some time at the weekend and prepare healthy food for lunches that you can freeze and pull out later. You can save more and eat more healthily by swapping meat for vegetables and pulses, which are nourishing sources of fibre, vitamins and minerals.

Leftovers from dinner are perfectly acceptable for lunch the next day and they don't require any planning. Just make an extra portion or two of everything when you cook your evening meal and put it in a portable container for reheating at work.

If you take hot soup in a vacuum flask, you'll avoid the lunchtime queue at the office microwave.

Here are some suggestions for nourishing and delicious packed lunches in winter:

- Homemade soup with crackers or bread
- Wholegrain pitta bread with roasted vegetables and hummus (take a separate container and assemble at work)
- Hearty winter casseroles, stews or curries
- Small items to snack on through the day – fruit, nuts, hard-boiled eggs, carrot sticks, dried apricots, wholegrain crackers, low-fat yoghurt.

FEED YOUR SKIN

Among the individual foods that can benefit the health of your skin are blueberries, avocados, scallops and prawns.

Blueberries: These berries contain flavonoids, which help to neutralise free radicals and strengthen the collagen in the walls of the blood vessels in the eyes. They are also rich in vitamin C, which helps to keep the skin supplied with oxygen and nutrients.

Avocados: The skin-savers of the food world. They can be applied externally to moisturise dry, damaged skin or eaten for numerous complexion benefits. Avocados contain around 28 grams (1 ounce) of fat, which helps to plump out skin cells and provides the nourishment needed to prevent dryness and wrinkles. The monounsaturated oils can also reduce skin inflammation.

Scallops: These shellfish are high in protein and very low in fat. They contain significant amounts of omega-3 oils, which help to prevent heart disease and counteract inflammation. They are also good sources of minerals, including the antioxidants selenium and zinc. If you suffer from excessively dry or oily skin, or regularly develop spots, you may be deficient in zinc, which is vital for skin repair and renewal.

Prawns: These are ideal if your skin has lost some of its lustre and softness. Prawns contain copper, vital for creating collagen and springy elastin, which form the deeper layers of the skin. Copper also helps skin to absorb ultraviolet rays and contributes to an even, natural skin colour.

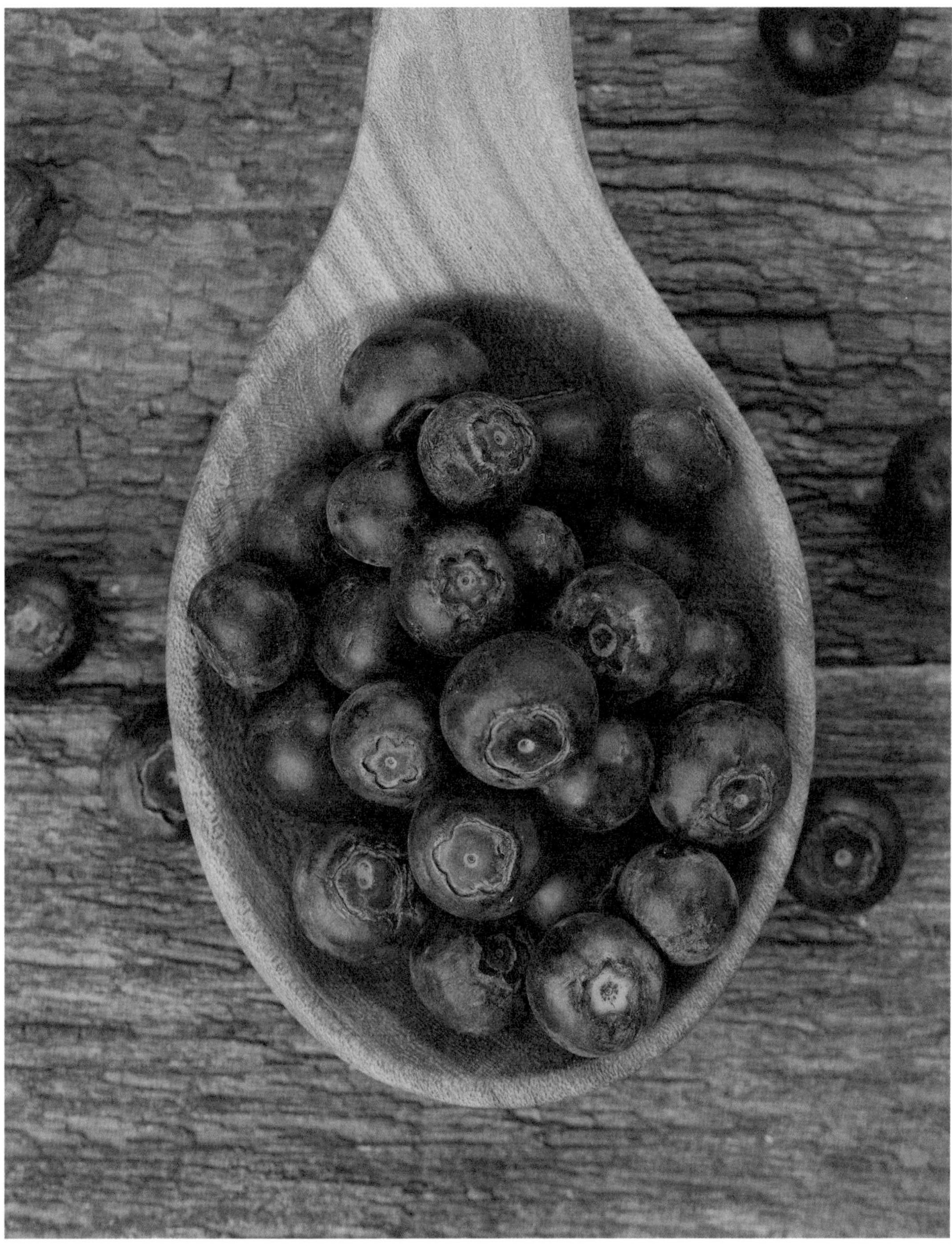

346

HAVE A SOCIAL MEDIA FAST

Using social media has become the norm for many of us, and with the expanding ways to document and advertise our lives through pictures and statuses we are observing each other through a rather skewed virtual lens. The way that people present themselves online is necessarily distorted, but it is easy to forget this and allow the information we see to impact our thoughts and mood, leaving us feeling despondent and demotivated about our own lives.

There's no denying the internet is an impressive source of information, but an overdose of the virtual at the expense of the real is not a good idea. Instead, enjoy privacy, focus on and be confident about your own life, and experience more of the world and people around you. So take a month off from checking your Facebook or Twitter account – you'll be surprised at how much you don't miss.

347

MAKE BEDTIME A LUXURY

A good night's sleep is crucial to your wellbeing, so make it a sublime experience by investing in high-quality bed linen. Natural fibres like linens and quality cottons are best because they are more breathable, long-lasting and environmentally friendly. Remember to change your sheets often to avoid attracting dust mites, which can trigger allergies. Once you've got the perfect sheets, dress your bed with blankets and throws in merino wool, mohair or cashmere for true indulgence. Then nestle in your luxurious bed linen and sleep tight.

348

MONITOR YOUR MINERALS

Besides playing a vital role in the healthy functioning of the body, minerals keep the immune system working well. Magic minerals include calcium for good bones, iron to transport oxygen in the blood, selenium to make certain enzymes, magnesium to help important biochemical reactions in the body and zinc to slow age-related deterioration of cells.

As we get older, we are more likely to become deficient in certain minerals and mineral deficiency may play a part in disease. For example, people with a lower magnesium intake are more likely to develop type-2 diabetes, while low levels of selenium are linked to poor immune function.

You get calcium from dairy products and fish such as salmon and sardines; iron from red meat, eggs, beans and leafy green vegetables; and zinc from meat and legumes.

349

MASTER SUDOKU

Sudoku is a wonderful way to exercise your brain – and there is something gently addictive about it. You don't need to be good at maths to solve a puzzle. In fact, the game doesn't really involve numbers – numbers are only used because they are well-recognised symbols.

There are dozens of different techniques you can use, but part of the pleasure of the game is working these out for yourself. Sudoku puzzles will make every journey on public transport pass more quickly, and they can even help you get to sleep at night. So next time you see sudoku puzzles in the paper or at a newsagent's stand, consider trying them out.

HEALTH DAY: BUTTERNUT SQUASH SOUP

Butternut squash, a member of the winter squash family, is an incredibly nutritious gourd that can be used in everything from soups to stir-fries. Squash is low in fat, high in fibre and chock full of nutrients and antioxidants like potassium, vitamin B6, vitamin C and carotenoids, which your body converts to the cancer-fighting vitamin A.

- 1 tablespoon olive oil
- 1 large onion, finely chopped
- 2 cloves garlic, crushed
- 2 large butternut squash, deseeded, peeled and diced
- 1½ teaspoons cumin
- 1 teaspoon fresh coriander
- ½ teaspoon ground nutmeg
- ¼ teaspoon chilli powder
- 1 teaspoon fresh thyme, chopped
- 3 vegetable stock cubes dissolved in 880 ml (3¾ cups) hot water
- fresh parsley and chives

Heat the oil in a large saucepan. Add the onion and garlic and cook over a low heat until the onion has softened. Add the squash, cumin, coriander, nutmeg, chilli, thyme and stock. Bring to a boil, reduce heat and simmer for 15 minutes. Season to taste and add the herbs.

Serves four.

351

BEWARE OF DRUGS

Many people believe that cannabis is a relatively harmless 'soft' drug, which can be beneficial for sufferers of various medical conditions. Evidence is mounting, however, that some forms of cannabis, such as skunk, can cause serious, long-term psychotic effects including paranoia, schizophrenia, anxiety and hallucinations. When the Institute of Psychiatry in London screened 280 hospital patients with psychotic symptoms, they found that nearly 80 per cent were heavy skunk users.

Individuals respond to drugs in different ways so, since it is impossible to predict which people are likely to fall victim to addiction or mental illness, it makes sense to avoid them altogether.

352

FIND FAITH

More than a thousand studies examining the effects of spirituality on healing have confirmed a link between religious observance and longevity of life. A 12-year study at the University of Iowa found that those who attended a religious service at least once a week were 35 per cent more likely to live longer than those who never attended such a service.

Being actively involved in a spiritual community – by attending a church, synagogue or mosque regularly, for example – is thought to boost the immune system and help to keep many age-related diseases at bay.

AVOID FOOD ADDITIVES

Nourish your body with food the way nature intended. The list of added nasties in food is extensive, but here are a few red alert additives to look out for:

What: Aspartame (E951). Artificial sweetener
Why: It is toxic and studies have shown it can affect cognitive function including intelligence and short-term memory.
Where: Diet or sugar-free sodas including Diet Coke and Coke Zero, baking goods, sugar-free breath mints, toothpaste

What: High fructose corn syrup, flavour enhancer
Why: Highly refined, said to be one of the biggest sources of calories in the USA, increases bad cholesterol, contributes to obesity and diabetes
Where: Soft drinks, sauces and dressings, baked beans, bread and pastry products, breakfast cereals, breakfast bars, processed snacks

What: Monosodium Glutamate (MSG, E621), flavour enhancer
Why: excitotoxin – overexcites taste bud cells to the point of damage or death, disengages the brain's 'I'm full' function
Where: Deep-fried fast foods, crisps, certain restaurant foods (ask if food contains MSG)

What: Sodium nitrate/nitrite. Preservative, colour and flavour enhancer
Why: Damages liver. The USDA tried to ban it in the 1970s but this was vetoed by food manufacturers.
Where: Bacon, corned beef, luncheon meats, hot dogs

What: Sulphur dioxide (E220), preservative
Why: Destroys vitamins B1 and E. Toxic, especially for people prone to asthma and high blood pressure. Can cause rashes and breathing difficulties
Where: Beer, wine, soft drinks, cordial, dried fruit

354

LOVE LIKE A BUDDHA

Loving kindness is a form of Buddhist meditation that aims to develop altruistic love while healing troubled minds. First you must learn to love yourself. Then you can direct feelings of loving kindness towards four chosen individuals: a figure of respect, such as a spiritual teacher; a close family member or friend; a neutral person; and a hostile person.

According to Buddhist teaching, if you send loving kindness from person to person in the above order, it will break down the barriers between the four people and yourself – and the effect will be to break down the divisions within your own mind. Visualise each person in turn and reflect on their positive qualities. Then make a positive statement about that person in your own words. Follow this by repeating an internalised mantra or phrase such as 'loving kindness'.

355

SEEK HELP (WHEN YOU NEED IT)

Modern counselling and psychotherapy can help relieve many types of psychological distress. It's especially useful if you are experiencing a difficult period and struggling to cope with issues on your own. There are many types of counselling available, from psychoanalytic therapy to cognitive-behavioural and group therapies. The goal is always to provide a non-judgemental environment where the client and therapist work together to resolve agreed issues. Take the time to find the right counsellor for you, ask for recommendations and do some research before committing. Seeking professional help is nothing to be ashamed of – just ask a New Yorker!

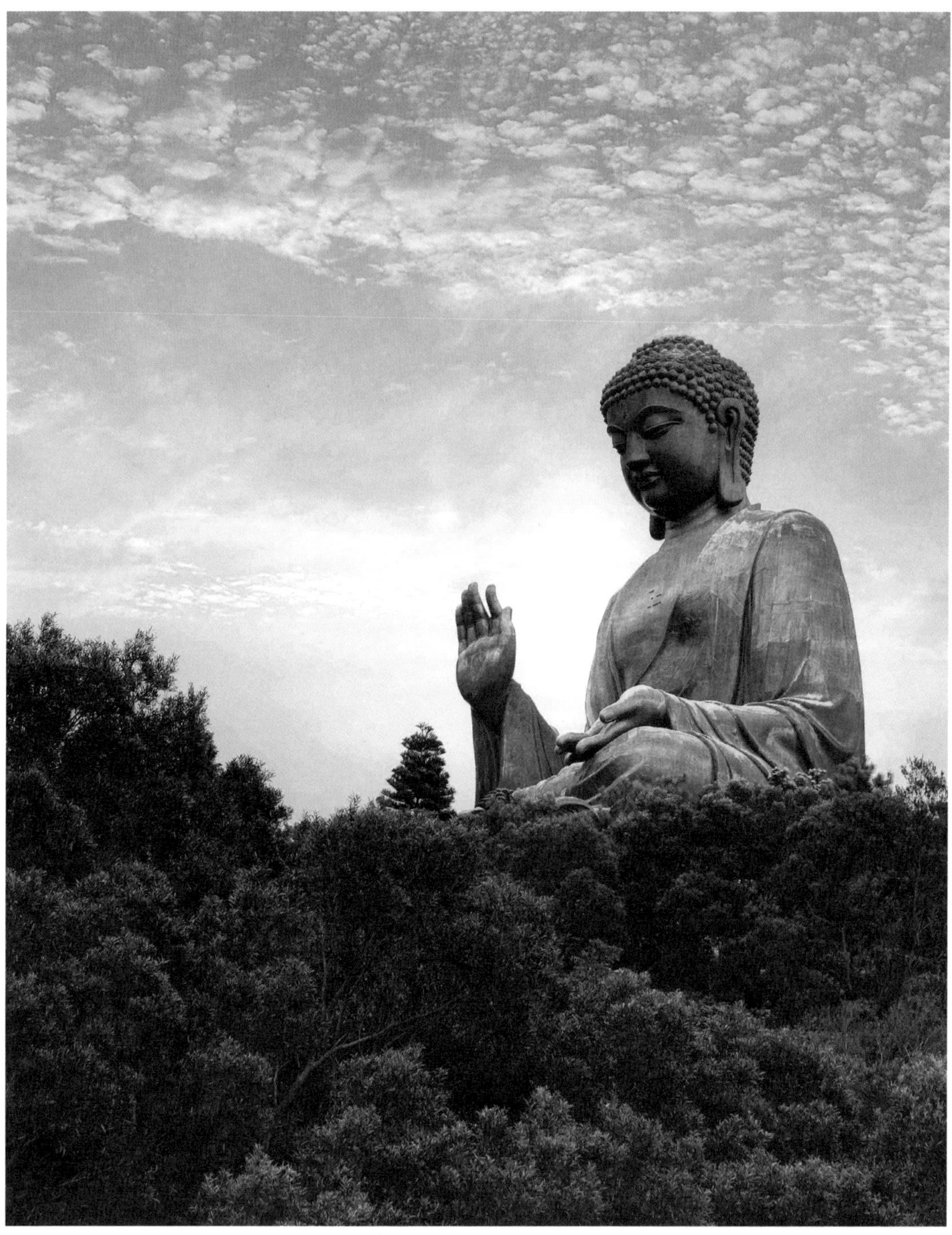

356

HAVE A GOOD SEX LIFE

When it comes to having sex, the current outlook stressed by therapists is for partners to focus on pleasure, mutuality and communication, rather than strictly on 'performance'. Using the term 'foreplay' suggests that it must lead up to something else. Intercourse then becomes a goal rather than a part of being sexual. So consider using the term 'outercourse' instead – the many sexual activities you and your partner can enjoy apart from having intercourse. Outercourse is pleasure-directed, rather than goal-directed, sexual activity. In other words, with no goals to pursue, partners can just have a good time.

To start with, try communicating better about sex. Feeling free to talk about what you like and want sexually really clears the air and turns your partner on. They're not a mind reader. Discuss how your repertoire can be expanded for mutual enjoyment. This may include watching some porn together and discussing what you found sexy or unsexy about it. It will make them feel accepted, too. Here are some ideas for spicing up your sex life:

- Look through a sexy lingerie catalogue together and have them tell you what they like about the model's bodies as well as what the models are – or are not – wearing.
- Make erotic promises. You can really light a fire with a few words about looking forward to a sexy time together.
- Get a video on sensual massage for the two of you to enjoy.
- Buy your partner a sex toy.
- Let them see you turned on. Being able to let yourself go when you are with your partner will arouse them.

357

STRETCH: QUADRICEPS

Tight legs can cause back problems and unbalanced leg muscles can cause issues with the knees and ankles. Regular stretching of the large muscles at the front of the thigh – the quadriceps – will help to realign the joints and keep them healthy.

- Lie on your stomach on the floor and bend one leg up behind you towards your buttock. Raise your upper body, resting on one elbow.
- Take your other hand and grasp the foot of your bent leg. Pull your foot gently into the buttock and hold. You will feel a stretch down the front of your thigh.
- Hold this pose for 15 seconds and then repeat on the other leg.

358

GIVE BACK

Volunteering is an incredibly fulfilling experience and it can benefit your own health and wellbeing as much as the people you help. Surveys have shown that volunteers enjoy lower stress levels than non-volunteers and more overall happiness and mental wellbeing. It can increase your self-confidence, expand your social network and skillset, strengthen your relationships and enrich your sense of purpose.

Once you've decided to volunteer, take the time to find the organisation with the best fit for your personality, talents and interests. There are literally hundreds to choose from, so make your efforts count by doing some research before you begin.

DAILY INSPIRATION

'You're braver than you believe, and stronger than you seem, and smarter than you think.'

Alan Alexander Milne
British author (1882–1956)

360

FEED YOUR NAILS

Healthy nails consist of 16 per cent water. When the level falls below this, nails become prone to brittleness, breakage and peeling. Foods that combat this deficiency include sweet peppers, herrings, garlic and black-eyed peas.

Peppers have a high water content, so they are particularly useful for keeping the skin and nails hydrated. They are also full of vitamin C, which helps to boost the immune system and fight fungal infections.

White spots on the nails may indicate a lack of vitamin E. Try adding some oats to your diet. Other good sources of vitamin E include pine nuts, sesame seeds and cashew nuts. Oats also contain iron, which helps to keep nails healthy and strong – a deficiency can lead to thin, brittle nails with a concave shape.

361

EAT WHOLEGRAIN

Grains are the seeds of cereal plants such as wheat, rye, barley, oats and rice. Wholegrains have three elements: a fibre-rich outer layer (the bran), a nutrient-packed inner layer (the germ) and a central starchy part (the endosperm). During processing, the bran and the germ are removed to give a 'whiter' refined cereal. Wholegrains, by contrast, retain all three layers with their concentration of nutrients.

Wholegrain foods include rolled oats, wholewheat breakfast cereals, wholemeal flour, brown rice, bulgur wheat and wholemeal, granary and multigrain breads.

FENG SHUI YOUR HOME

According to ancient Chinese belief, the five elements of feng shui – wood, fire, earth, water and metal – interact with each other in various ways, and each element is represented by a different colour or colours.

You can place colours or objects in such a way as to bring more harmony into your home, but before doing so you need to make an 'energy map' of each room. Use either:

- Compass readings to divide the space into eight – northeast, south, southwest, etc.

or

- A square grid consisting of nine smaller squares.

Each of the subdivisions of a space corresponds with a 'life area', such as health or family, as well as a feng shui element and colour.

You can work to improve one area of your life by introducing an appropriate 'cure'. If you want to enhance the love and marriage energy, and you have found a perfect feng shui cure for love – a sculpture of lovers embracing, for example – you should place the object in the southwest sector (the love and marriage feng shui area, according to classical tradition).

363

DISCOVER THE SECRETS OF GINSENG

The root of the ginseng plant has been used in Chinese medicine for thousands of years to promote longevity and good health. In modern times it has been shown to boost the immune system and to combat the physical effects of stress.

Usually taken in capsule form as a health supplement, ginseng stimulates the production of T-cells, which destroy harmful viruses and bacteria. It also regulates the release in the body of stress hormones and benefits the hormone-producing organs such as the pituitary gland and the adrenal glands. Herbalists believe that ginseng can relieve fatigue and increase energy, and some athletes take it to enhance stamina. However, people with high blood pressure should not take ginseng.

364

THINK CRITICALLY

Critical thinking can improve your academic performance by helping you to understand and evaluate the arguments and views of others and develop your own perspective. To analyse a new situation, you need to think clearly and critically about the facts in front of you. Here are a couple of tips for developing critical thinking:

- Be questioning. Think things through rather than accepting them at face value.
- Focus on the facts. Rather than blindly following theories, pay attention to the information that you yourself have gathered and analyse what it tells you.

LIVE IT UP!

Congratulations! You have reached the end of your journey through a year of wellbeing. By now you should be well on the way to becoming healthier, happier and smarter.

We hope that with the skills and advice we have presented in these pages, you will be inspired, informed and better equipped to face life's pleasures and challenges.

Life is short so make it count by enjoying the changing seasons with all they have to offer. Nurture your health. Exercise your body and your mind. Take the time to do the things you love. Remember, there are 365 days in every single year and each one is an opportunity to grow in wisdom, strength and happiness.

And if there are any subjects in the book that interest you particularly, follow them up and search for more information. You never know where they might take you...

INDEX

FURTHER READING

This reading list is organised into broader wellbeing topics with general resources listed first, followed by the studies and articles discussed throughout the book.

Nutrition
www.bbcgoodfood.com
www.eatingwell.com

Mattson, M.P. 'Neuroprotective signaling and the aging brain: take away my food and let me run.' *Brain Research.* 2000; 886(1–2):47–53.

Mattson, M.P., Duan, W., Guo, Z. 'Meal size and frequency affect neuronal plasticity and vulnerability to disease: cellular and molecular mechanisms.' *Journal of Neurochemistry.* 2003; 84(3):417–31.

Morgan, T.E., Wong A.M., Finch C.E. 'Anti-inflammatory mechanisms of dietary restriction in slowing aging processes.' *Interdisciplinary Topics in Gerontology.* 2007; 35:83–97.

DeKosky, S.T., et al. 'Ginkgo biloba for prevention of dementia.' *Journal of the American Medical Association.* 2008; 300:2253–62.

Organic food: www.theguardian.com/uk/2006/sep/02/supermarkets.fooddanddrink; http://news.bbc.co.uk/1/hi/business/6973352.stm

Clarke, R., Armitage, J. 'Antioxidant vitamins and risk of cardiovascular disease. Review of large-scale randomised trials.' *Cardiovascular Drugs and Therapy* (sponsored by the International Society of Cardiovascular Pharmacotherapy). 2002; 16(5):411–5.

Benton, D. & Parker, P. 'Breakfast, blood glucose and cognition.' *American Journal of Clinical Nutrition.* 1998; 67 Suppl: 772S.

Knarek, R. 'Psychological effects of snacks and altered meal frequency.' *British Journal of Nutrition.* 1997;77 Suppl 1:S105–S120.

Smith, A., et al 'Effects of evening meal and caffeine on cognitive performance, mood and cardiovascular functioning the following day.' *Journal of Psychopharmacology.* 1993; 7:203–206.

Akbaraly, N.T., Arnaud, J., Hininger-Favier, I., et al. 'Selenium and mortality in the elderly: results from the EVA study.' *Clinical Chemistry.* 2005; 51(11):2117–23.

Pawelec, G., Ouyang, Q., Wagner, W., et al. 'Pathways to a robust immune response in the elderly.' *Immunology and Allergy Clinics of North America.* 2003; 23(1):1–13.

Body
www.livestrong.com
www.bbc.co.uk/news/health

Gillespie, L.D., Gillespie, W.J., et al. 'Interventions for preventing falls in elderly people.' *Cochrane Database of Systematic Reviews.* 2003; 4.

Smyth, B., Fan, J., Hser, Y.I. 'Life expectancy and productivity loss among narcotics addicts thirty-three years after index treatment.' *Journal of Addictive Diseases.* 2006; 25(4):37–47.

Ames, B.N., Shigenaga, M.K., Hagen, T.M., et al. 'Oxidants, antioxidants, and the degenerative diseases of aging.' *Proc Natl Acad Sci USA.* 1993; 90:7915–22.

Doll, R., Richards, P., Boreham, J. & Sutherland, I. 'Mortality in relation to smoking: 50 years' observations on male British doctors.' *British Medical Journal.* 2004; 328:1519.

Hughes, J. R., Shiffman, S., Callas, P., Zhang, J. 'A meta-analysis of the efficacy of over-the-counter nicotine replacement.' *Tobacco Control.* 2003; 12:21–7.

Law, M., Wald, N. 'Why heart disease mortality is low in France: the time lag explanation.' *British Medical Journal.* 1999; 318:1471–80.

Kado, D.M., Huang, M.H., Karlamangla, A.S., et al. 'Hyperkyphotic posture predicts mortality in older community – dwelling men and women: a prospective study.' *Journal of the American Geriatrics Society.* 2004; 52(10):1662–7.

The American Academy of Periodontology. 'Tooth or consequences: 10 steps to add years to your life.' 2005; http://www.perio.org/consumer/addyears.htm.

Beck, J. et al. 'Periodontal disease and cardiovascular disease.' *Journal of Periodontology.* 1996; 67(suppl 10):1123–37.

Chattha, R., et al, 'Effect of yoga on cognitive functions in climacteric syndrome: a randomized control study.' *British Journal of Obstetrics and Gynaecology.* 2008; 115:991–1000.

Virtanen, M., et al, 'Long working hours and cognitive function.' *American Journal of Epidemiology.* 2009.

Cirelli, C. 'Sleep disruption, oxidative stress, and aging: new insights from fruit flies.' *Proceedings of the National Academy of Sciences of the United States of America.* 2006; 103(38):13901–02.

Tafaro, L., Cicconetti, P., et al. 'Sleep quality of centenarians: cognitive and survival implications.' *Archives of Gerontology and Geriatrics.* 2007; 44S:385–9.

Hamilton, N. A., Gallagher, M.W. & Preacher, K. J. 'Insomnia and well-being.' *Journal of Consulting and Clinical Psychology.* 2007; 75(6):939–946.

Hamilton, N. A., Nelson, C., Stevens, N. & Kitzman, H. 'Sleep and psychological well-being.' *Social Indicators Research.* 2007; 82:147–163.

Kidneys: www.esciencenews.com/articles/2008/11/06/kidney.transplantation.provides.cognitive.benefits.patients.with.kidney.disease.

Hailpern, S.M., et al. 'Moderate chronic kidney disease and cognitive function in adults 20 to 59 years of age: third national health and nutrition examination survey.' *Journal of the American Society of Nephrology.* 2007; 18:2205–2213.

Hayashi, M., et al, 'The effects of a 20 min nap in the mid-afternoon on mood, performance and EEG activity.' *Clinical Neurophysiology.* 1999; 110:272–279.

Tietzel, A.J., Lack, L.C., 'The short-term benefits of brief and long naps following nocturnal sleep restriction.' *Sleep.* 2001; 24:293–300.

Mind
www.psychologytoday.com
www.meditationmojo.com/meditation-articles
www.brainmetrix.com

Kashdan, T.B. & Roberts, J.E. 'Affective outcomes in superficial and intimate interactions: Roles of social anxiety and curiosity.' *Journal of Research in Personality.* 2006; 40(2):140–167.

Park, N., Peterson, C. & Seligman, M.E.P. 'Strengths of character and well-being.' *Journal of Social & Clinical Psychology.* 2004; 23(5): 603–619.

Peterson, C. *A Primer in Positive Psychology.* New York: Oxford University Press. 2006; 137–164.
Liptrap JM, et al. 'Chess and standard test scores.' *Chess Life.* 1998; March:41–43.
Wilson, R.S., Scherr, P.A., Schneider, J.A., Tang, Y., Bennett, D.A.'The relation of cognitive activity to risk of developing Alzheimer's disease.' *Neurology.* 2007.
Lyubomirsky, S & Ross, L. 'Hedonic consequences of social comparison: A contrast of happy and unhappy people.' *Journal of Personality and Social Psychology.* 1997; 73(6):1141–1157.
Kubzansky, L.D., Sparrow, D., Vokonas ,P., Kawachi, I. 'Is the glass half empty or half full? A prospective study of optimism and coronary heart disease in the normative aging study.' *Psychosomatic Medicine.* 2001; 63:910–916.
Maruta, T., Colligan, R.C., Malinchoc, M. & Offord, K.P. 'Optimism-pessimism assessed in the 1960s and self-reported health status 30 years later.' *Mayo Clinic Proceedings.* 2002; 77:748–753.
Bauer, J.J. & McAdams, D.P. 'Growth goals, maturity and well-being.' *Developmental Psychology.* 2004; 40(1):114–127.
Kwan, C.M.L, Love, G. D., Ryff, C.D. & Essex, M.J. 'The role of self-enhancing evaluations in a successful life transition.' *Psychology and Aging.* 2003; 18(1):3–12.
Griffiths, S. 'The experience of creative activity as a treatment medium.' *Journal of Mental Health.* 2008; 17(1):49–63.
Nettle, D. *Happiness: The Science Behind Your Smile.* Oxford: Oxford University Press. 2006.
Maddux, J.E. 'Self-efficacy: The power of believing you can.' In C.R. Snyder & S.J. Lopez (Eds.), *Handbook of Positive Psychology.* New York: Oxford University Press. 2002; 277–287.
Pellegrini, A.D., Dupuis, D. & Peter K. 'Play in evolution and development.' *Developmental Review.* 2007; 27(2):261–276.
Sternberg, R.J., Kaufman, J.C. and Grigorenko, E.L. *Applied Intelligence.* Cambridge: Cambridge University Press. 2008.
Martin, R.A. 'Humor, laughter, and physical health: Methodological issues and research findings.' *Psychological Bulletin.* 2001; 127(4):504–519.
Skevington, S.M. & White, A.'Is laughter the best medicine?' *Psychology & Health.* 1998; 13(1):157–169.
Neuhoff, C.C. & Schaefer, C. 'Effects of laughing, smiling, and howling on mood.' *Psychological Reports.* 2002; 91(3):1079–1080.
Csikszentmihalyi, M. *Flow.* London: Rider. 2002.
Goleman, D. *Emotional Intelligence: Why It Can Matter More Than IQ.* London: Bloomsbury. 1996.
Withnall, A. & Thompson, V. 'Older people and lifelong learning: choices and experiences.' 2002; www.tlrp.org/project%20sites/withnall.
Soussignan, R. 'Duchenne smile, emotional experience, and autonomic reactivity: A test of the facial feedback hypothesis.' *Emotion.* 2002; 2(1):52–74.
Clow, A. & Fredhoi, C. 'Normalisation of salivary cortisol levels and self-report stress by a brief lunch-time visit to an art gallery by London City workers.' *Journal of Holistic Healthcare.* 2006; 3(2).
Baumeister, R.F. & Vohs, K.D. *Handbook of Self-Regulation: Research, Theory and Applications.* New York: Guilford Press. 2004.
Dweck, C.S. *Mindset: The New Psychology of Success.* New York: Random House. 2006.
Macan, T. H. 'Time-management training: Effects on time behaviors, attitudes and job performance.' *Journal of Psychology: Interdisciplinary and Applied.* 1996; 130(3): 229–236.
Bryant, F.B. & Veroff, J. *Savoring: A new model of positive experience.* Mahwah, New Jersey: Lawrence Erlbaum Associates Publishers. 2007.
Collins, J. *Good to Great: Why some companies make the leap…and others don't.* London: Random House. 2001.
King, L.A. & Hicks, J.A. 'Whatever happened to "What might have been"? Regrets, happiness, and maturity.' *American Psychologist.* 2007; 62(7):625–636.
Video games: www.abcnews.go.com/wnt/health/story?id=814080.
Foster, K.M. & Reeves, C.K. 'Foreign language in the elementary school improves cognitive skills.' *FLES News.* 1989; 2:4.
Samuels, D.D. & Griffore, R.J. 'The Plattsburgh French language immersion program: its influence on intelligence and self esteem.' *Language Learning.* 1979; 29:45–52.
Fredrickson, B.L., Tugade, M.M., Waugh, C.E. & Larkin, G.R. 'What good are positive emotions in crisis? A prospective study of resilience and emotions following the terrorist attacks on the United States on September 11th, 2001.' *Journal of Personality and Social Psychology.* 2003; 84(2):365–376.
Linley, P.A., & Joseph, S. 'Positive changes following trauma and adversity: a review.' *Journal of Traumatic Stress Studies.* 2004; 17:11–21.
Pennebaker, J.W. & Beall, S.K. 'Confronting a traumatic event: Toward an understanding of inhibition and disease.' *Journal of Abnormal Psychology.* 1986; 95(3):274–281.
Sheffield, D., Duncan, E. & Thomson, K. 'Written emotional expression and well-being: Result from a home-based study.' *Australasian Journal of Disaster and Trauma Studies.* 2002; 6(1).
Curry, L.A., Snyder, C. R. & Cook, D.L. 'Role of hope in academic and sport achievement.' *Journal of Personality and Social Psychology.* 1997; 73(6):1257–1267.
Lopez, S.J., Snyder, C.R., Magyar-Moe, J.L., Edwards, L.M., Pedrotti, J.T., Janowski, K., Turner, J.L., Pressgrove, C. & Hackman, A. 'Strategies for Accentuating Hope.' In. P.A. Linley & S. Joseph (Eds.) *Positive Psychology in Practice.* 2004;388–404.
Halpern, D.F. 'Teaching critical thinking for transfer across domains.' *American Psychologist* 1998; 53:449–455.
Lucas, R., Clark, A., Georgellis, Y. & Diener, E. 'Unemployment Alters the Set-Point for Life Satisfaction.' *Psychological Science.* 2004; 15:8–13.

Social

www.succeedsocially.com

Gable, S.L., Reis, H.T., Impett, E.A. & Asher, E.R. 'What Do You Do When Things Go Right? The Intrapersonal and Interpersonal Benefits of Sharing Positive Events.' *Journal of Personality and Social Psychology.* 2004; 87(2):228–245.
Langston, C. A. 'Capitalizing on and coping with daily-life events: Expressive responses to positive events.' *Journal of Personality and Social Psychology.* 1994; 67:1112–1125.
Gardner, J. & Oswald, A. 'How is mortality affected by money, marriage and stress?' *Journal of Health Economics.* 2004; 23(6):1181–1207
Kaplan, R.M. & Kronick, R.G. 'Marital status and longevity in the United States population.' *Journal of Epidemiology and Community Health.* 2006; 60(9):760–5.
Memory: www.nytimes.com/2008/05/13/health/13brain.html.

Social intelligence: www.pnas.org/content/99/7/4436.abstract.

McCullough, M.E. & Witvliet, C.V. 'The psychology of forgiveness.' C.R. Snyder, Shane J. Lopez. (Eds.) *Handbook of Positive Psychology.* New York: Oxford University Press. 2002; 446–458.

Witvliet, C. V., Ludwig, T.E. & Vander Laan, K.L. 'Granting forgiveness or harboring grudges: Implications for emotion, physiology and health.' *Psychological Science.* 2001; 12(2):117–123.

Tucker, C.J., McHale, S.M. & Crouter, A.C. 'Conflict resolution: Links with adolescents' family relationships and individual well-being.' *Journal of Family Issues* 2003; 24(6):715–736.

Wells, D.L. 'Domestic dogs and human health: An overview.' *British Journal of Health Psychology.* 2007; 12(1):145–156.

Allen, K., Blascovich, J. & Mendes, W.B. 'Cardiovascular reactivity and the presence of pets, friends, and spouses: the truth about cats and dogs.' *Psychosomatic Medicine.* Sept–Oct 2002; 64(5):727–39.

Friedmann, E. & Thomas, S.A. 'Pet ownership, social support, and one-year survival after acute myocardial infarction in the Cardiac Arrhythmia Suppression Trial (CAST).' *American Journal of Cardiology.* Dec 1995; 15:76(17):1213–7.

Siegel, J.M. 'Stressful life events and use of physician services among the elderly: the moderating role of pet ownership.' *Journal of Personality and Social Psychology.* 1990; 58(6):1081–6.

Smith, V. 'In pursuit of good sex: Self determination and the sexual experience.' *Journal of Social and Personal Relationships.* 2007; Vol.24:69–85.

Helliwell, J. F. & Putnam, R. D. 'The social context of wellbeing.' F.A. Huppert, N. Baylis, B. Keverne (Eds.) *The Science of Well-being.* New York: Oxford University Press. 2005; 435–459.

Diener, E. & Seligman, M.E.P. 'Very happy people.' *Psychological Science.* 2002; 13(1): 81–84.

Peterson, C. *A Primer in Positive Psychology.* New York: Oxford University Press. 2006.

Sheldon, K. M. & Lyubomirsky, S. 'Achieving Sustainable New Happiness: Prospects, Practices and Prescriptions.' P.A. Linley & S. Joseph (Eds.) *Positive psychology in practice.* Hoboken, New Jersey: John Wiley & Sons Inc. 2004; 127–145.

Koenig, H. (Ed.) *A Handbook of Religion and Mental Health.* Burlington, Massachusetts: Academic Press. 1998.

Environment

www.goodhousekeeping.com
www.yourguidetogreen.com

Burns, G.W. (2005). 'Naturally happy, naturally healthy: the role of the natural environment in well-being.' F.A.Huppert, N. Baylis and B. Keverne (Eds.) *The Science of Well-being.* New York: Oxford University Press. 2005; 405–431.

Dasgupta, P. *Human Well-being and the Natural Environment.* New York: Oxford University Press. 2001.

Hartig, T., Evans, G. W., Jamner, L. D., Davis, D. S. & Gärling, T. Tracking restoration in natural and urban field settings. *Journal of Environmental Psychology.* 2003; 23:109–123.

Gigliotti, C.M. & Jarrott, S.E. 'Effects of Horticulture Therapy on Engagement and Affect.' *Canadian Journal on Aging.* 2005; 24(4):367–377.

Heliker, D., Chadwick, A. & O'Connell, T. 'The meaning of gardening and the effects on perceived well being of a gardening project on diverse populations of elders.' *Activities, Adaptation & Aging.* 2000; 24(3):35–56.

Plastic bags: http://news.nationalgeographic.com/news/2003/09/0902_030902_plasticbags.html.

Trees: www.arborday.org/globalwarming/.

Harvesting rainwater: www.savetherain.info/media-centre/rainwater-harvesting-faqs.aspx.

Stoyke, G. *The Carbon Buster's Home Energy Handbook.* Gabriola Island, British Columbia: New Society Publishers. 2006.

Clothes washing: www.energystar.gov/index.cfm?c=clotheswash.pr_clothes_washers.

Public transport: www.apta.com:80/resources/reportsandpublications/Pages/EnergyEnvironment.aspx.

Okinawan Centenarian Study: www.okicent.org/cent.html.

Diener, E. & Seligman, M.E.P. 'Beyond money: toward an economy of well-being.' *Psychological Science in the Public Interest.* 2004; 5(1):1–31.

Lee, I.M. et al. 'Exercise intensity and longevity in men. The Harvard Alumni health study.' *Journal of the American Medical Association.* 1995; 273(15).

Energy saving tips: www.energysavingtrust.org.uk/Take-action/Energy-saving-top-tips.

Roges, L. 'Architects role in shedding light on solar power design.' *Real Estate Weekly*, 8 August 2007.

Heating: www.aceee.org/consumer/heating.

Epperson, C.N., Terman, M., Terman, J.S., Hanusa, B.H., Oren, D.A., Peindl, K.S. & Wisner, K.L. 'Randomized clinical trial of bright light therapy for antepartum depression: preliminary findings.' *Journal of Clinical Psychiatry.* 2004; 65:421–425.

Grant, W.B. & Holick, M.F. 'Benefits and requirements of vitamin D for optimal health: A review.' *Alternative Medicine Review.* 2005; 10 (2):94–111.

Holick, M.F. 'Vitamin D: important for prevention of osteoporosis, cardiovascular heart disease, type 1 diabetes, autoimmune diseases, and some cancers.' *Southern Medical Journal* 2005; 98(10):1024–27.

Holick M.F. 'Sunlight and vitamin D for bone health and prevention of autoimmune diseases, cancers, and cardiovascular disease.' *American Journal of Clinical Nutrition.* 2004; 80 suppl. 6:1678S–88S.

City vs nature: www.boston.com/bostonglobe/ideas/articles/2009/01/04/how_the_city_hurts_your_brain; www.sciencedaily.com/releases/2009/02/090217092758.htm.